# A FIELD GUIDE
## FOR FOLLOWERS OF CHRIST

### KEITH MARTENS, M. Div.

### Kingdom Ministries International

*To Jou*

*& Becky!*

*so blessed & proud*
*of you both for your lives*
*& service in God's Kingdom.*
*I hope you find this helpful*
*in your personal lives & ministry*

*Much love.*

*Uncle Beef*

Published by Perfect Marketing Team, Fresno, CA
Design and layout by Nancy Avera
Printed in the United States of America

## DEDICATED TO MY BIGGEST FANS

Joanie, my more than patient wife.

Our amazing staff who faithfully
encourage, support, and serve.

## FOR

Christ and His Kingdom

## SPECIAL THANKS TO

Carrie Alcorn and Cathy Crosby, my personal
grammar police, Robin Turner and Shawna Short.
Nancy Avera and Marci Bertalotto for making this
happen. For those on the front line and those willing to be.

## TRY IT FIRST

Then, call or contact us with your questions.

Let us know your stories, testimonies, and the ways we
can support you in advancing the Kingdom of God and
living a life of discipleship under the Lordship of Jesus
Christ as a dynamic part of His Body, the church.

www.**Kingdom**Ministries**Intl**.org

# WHAT OTHERS ARE SAYING

James G. Friesen, Ph.D. – *Clinical Psychologist & Author*

*"Keith has been a trusted friend since last century. He is a prime mover in God's Kingdom. Here is how God's Kingdom works: The Father is constantly at work to bestow grace on all of His children. He gives His leaders a vision about how to pass along that grace, and it is up to them to bring that vision to life. Keith is one of His visionary leaders. This Field Guide will spread His grace far and wide. Thanks, Keith, for this grace-producing tool. May it advance His Kingdom."*

---

Danny Lehmann, Dean, College of Christian Ministries
*University of the Nations, Youth With A Mission*

*"At our Youth With A Mission missionary training base in Honolulu, we have had the privilege of partaking of Keith Marten's ministry for several years. Our students come from various backgrounds and many of them come in wounded, abused, and often anemic in their power to overcome some of the most basic temptations and weaknesses they face.*

*Keith has had years of experience in setting the captives free with a refreshing and simple mixture of belief in the Bible as God's Word and the power and the authority given us in Jesus' name as ambassadors and then being able to use that authority to affect change in people's lives. We have seen Keith do this over and over as he and his teams have come to minister to our young students. I would highly recommend his Field Guide as a manual for your own work among this generation of zealous but sometimes wounded individuals. Freedom is waiting for them in the name of Jesus, if administered by people who understand the authority they have in that name. Keith is bold in asserting that God's power is still available to us today."*

Alan Doswald, Executive Director – **Evangelicals for Social Action**

> *"Kingdom Ministries ... is a powerful and unique ministry to equip believers to understand and use their spiritual authority to pray for others and set them free in Christ. I know of several people who have experienced profound healing through Kingdom Ministries."*

---

Pastor Roger Whitlow – **Valley Christian Center Fresno**

> *"This ministry is a gift to the body of Christ and it needs to find its way into Valley churches.*
>
> *There are people sitting in church who are desperate to receive what this ministry can offer so that they can be free to take their place in the body of Christ and be all that God has called them to be.*
>
> *I can't think of a greater gift to a pastor than to have lay people equipped to minister; to have lay-led teams ministering to people in need within the church body. I feel that the Lord said to me that He wants Kingdom Ministries to grow beyond what I can imagine. I feel that is a prophetic word from the Lord and I ask that you agree with me for this."*

---

Pastor Tom Parsons
**Retired from First Presbyterian Church, Fresno**

> *"I've been involved in healing ministry for the past 30 years and been trained to do this about four different ways, but I found the way Keith is teaching is unique."*

*"What I appreciate about this ministry is the dependence on the Holy Spirit's leading – asking Jesus to show the client what's going on and the insights that come through the Holy Spirit revealing step by step how to bring freedom and healing. I am sold that this is the most effective way to do ministry.*

*I have seen lives changed in significant ways; my own life has changed significantly.*

*I really pray that this ministry will expand because it has been such a service to our church."*

---

Pastor Greg Tawlks – *Olive Branch Church, Sacramento*

*"They really taught us to listen to God and allow Him to counsel and how to minister to people and teach them to listen to God and hear His voice for themselves.*

*Keith came with a team to our church to teach us how to pray and minister to those in our church. They just poured out to us. I came down from Sacramento to speak at this event because I so appreciate this ministry.*

*We're so excited that our people are learning how to pray and minister to each other."*

# SECTION I

## ORIENTATION

# SECTION II

## THE NATURE AND PRACTICE OF BIBLICAL AND EFFECTIVE PRAYER

# SECTION III

## KINGDOM EVANGELISM AND OUTREACH

# CONCLUSION

## FINAL THOUGHTS

# FOREWORD

Thank you for your interest in pursuing a life of discipleship under the Lordship of Jesus Christ to advance His Kingdom on earth. This material is designed to help you live and minister effectively in the manner of Jesus and His disciples. Our goal is to enable you to minister with others as a uniquely gifted member of Christ's Body, the Church.

This Field Guide is a handy resource you can take with you anywhere. It contains instructions for personal ministry and is a helpful and convenient guide for individual or small group use in personal ministry settings, in evangelism and missions outreach, on prayer teams, or in settings where you have the opportunity to minister to individuals with the love and power of Christ.

The primary emphasis is upon the person and ministry of the Lord Jesus Christ who is both present in us and with us when we gather in His Name. Therefore, the material provided in this Field Guide is not a program or series of steps to follow. We pray it will guide you into having a dynamic and interactive encounter with Jesus Christ through the

> We pray this book will guide you into a dynamic and interactive encounter with Jesus Christ through the counsel and empowerment of the Holy Spirit.

counsel and empowerment of the Holy Spirit along with others He has gifted in His Body, the Church. You will be able to experientially participate with Jesus in His life and ministry of proclaiming the Good News and seeing others set free.

From observing the Gospel accounts, we see that the most essential characteristics of Jesus' life and ministry that we must understand and practice are:

- Consistent and purposeful dependence on the Father through the Holy Spirit's counsel and empowerment.

- Expressions of authority and power evident in His teaching, healing, and encounters with Satan and the Kingdom of darkness.

- Obedience to the Father to advance His Kingdom through the declaration and assertion of God's truth.

Similarly, in the Book of Acts we observe how the early church continues the ministry of Jesus. They, too, demonstrated a vital dependence on the Holy Spirit to empower and guide them in every area of life. Instead of a simplistic presentation of Gospel or a programmatic approach to evangelism, we see these early disciples continuing the same ministry Jesus began – preaching not only the message about Jesus but the Good News of the Kingdom which was central to Jesus' teaching. They also continued Jesus' ministry and the commission He gave them to heal the sick, cast out demons and raise the dead as part of their message of the Good News. Their message, as the Apostle Paul says, was given with not only words but with a demonstration of the Spirit's power that led to believing faith. The power and authority of Christ is now available to all believers through the Holy Spirit who was sent to them (Acts 1:8; 3:1-9;13:9-12;16:16-18).

# SECTION I

ORIENTATION TO THE FIELD
GUIDE FOR FOLLOWERS OF
CHRIST

ORIENTATION

# ORIENTATION

When asked the question, "To which direction does the needle of a compass point?" most people will respond with the seemingly obvious answer, "north." While this may be correct in a general sense, it is incorrect in regard to "True North." To determine True North one must, depending upon where they are located, adjust their compass and course of travel by calculating the difference between Magnetic North and a geographic area called Magnetic North. Even in a relatively short distance of 10 miles the failure to do so will result in missing one's precise destination.

In the same way, we often find ourselves guided by our emotions and desires rather than the truth of God's Word. There are times, for example, we may repeatedly ask God's forgiveness because we feel bad because of what we have done; or because we do not feel forgiven. However, the truth is, *"When we admit our sin, God can be relied upon to forgive us for our sins and to cleanse us from all unrighteousness"* **1 John 1:9.** Despite how we feel we can accept or adjust to God's truth then determine our course of direction by living and acting according to His truth. This, rather than our feelings, will lead us in the path to freedom and righteousness. May this Field Guide serve as an instrument to assist you and others to walk in the truth and pursue the freedom Christ promised and secured for us at the cross.

The foundation for a life of discipleship and ministry include the following three principles that are outlined in the first three chapters of this guide.

1. Relying on the Holy Spirit's counsel and power

2. Utilizing Jesus' power and authority as an ambassador of Christ

3. Declaring and asserting God's truth

# RELYING ON THE HOLY SPIRIT'S COUNSEL AND POWER

Like Jesus, the disciples lived, ministered, and were guided and empowered by the Holy Spirit in very practical ways. They were empowered to understand, speak, and preach God's Word, to heal the sick, and to free people from the influences of Satan and the power of sin. They were also guided, warned, and made decisions as a result of His counsel and leading. In this Field Guide we will rely on the Holy Spirit's counsel and power in the following ways:

- To guide us into truth, and to lead and counsel us.

- For direction and discernment when gathered together in His presence.

- To pray and minister in the power of God.

- To live in obedience and walk in the light of His truth.

- To remain in Christ and rely on Him and His resources.

- To uncover the origin of negative patterns of thinking, feeling and behavior.

- To recognize and acknowledge the truth about what is, what has happened and how we feel.

---

- To reveal, experience, and heal our emotions.

- To live in and minister the freedom of Christ to others.

Jesus and His disciples clearly model for us a lifestyle of relying on the Spirit of God in them and with them, as they follow Christ and carry out His mission. In the Book of Acts we observe the inter-action between the early believers and the Holy Spirit, as they are learning to live for the first time without the physical presence of Jesus among them. We notice the ways Jesus communicates with them through the Holy Spirit, as they gather to inquire of Him and purpose to live for Him.

> The term *Interactive Prayer* will be used to describe the personal dialogue or interaction we have with God, through the presence of the Holy Spirit, the person(s) we are praying with and ourselves.

The term ***Interactive Prayer*** will be used to describe the personal dialogue or interaction we have with God, through the presence of the Holy Spirit, the person(s) we are praying with and ourselves. We are asking God, who is present by His Spirit, to lead and counsel us as we go. As we ask, we learn to listen and respond to His counsel and what He reveals to those involved. The foundation for this approach are the words and ministry of Jesus Christ characterized in the Gospel of John, chapter 16.

*"But when He, the Spirit of truth, comes, He will guide you into all truth. He will not speak on His own; He will speak only what He hears, and He will tell you what is yet to come. He will bring glory to Me by taking from what is Mine and making it known to you. All that belongs to the Father is Mine. That is why I said the Spirit will take from what is Mine and make it known to you."* **John 16:13-15**

# 2

# UTILIZING JESUS' POWER AND AUTHORITY AS AN AMBASSADOR OF CHRIST

As an ambassador of Christ we will use the authority and power of Jesus in the following ways:

- To assert Christ's Lordship, dominion, and will over evil and it's influence.

- To advance God's purpose and will on earth and in every place and situation of life.

- To reclaim that which rightfully belongs to God and is held captive by Satan and his power.

- To cancel the effects of unrighteous acts, lies, and influences of evil.

- To verbally address, expose, test, and resolve spiritual influences of evil.

- To verbally declare God's truth and will.

- By speaking directly to sickness and unseen influences of evil in Jesus' Name.

Utilizing the authority of Christ is a declaration of God's truth and includes speaking in the name of Jesus as we see in Jesus' and the disciples' ministry (Luke 4:39; John 5:8; Acts 3:6; 16:18, etc.)  By contrast, intercessory prayer is appealing to God with requests and petitions. Speaking for God and to God are both important to effectively pray for people in need and for advancing the purposes of God.

## A BIBLICAL DEFINITION OF AUTHORITY

Authority as characterized in the New Testament and expressed in the ministries of Jesus and His disciples is the ability, right, or power to do something. This ability or power is derived from another person or source and is given to someone for a particular purpose. In the New Testament there is a clear association of being empowered and filled with the Holy Spirit, and the expression of authority to minister and carry out God's purpose on earth. (Luke 3,4, 24:49; Acts 1:8; 4:31) To continue the work of Jesus and to express His will on earth, one must go beyond simply believing to ACTING on the authority Christ has given us.

> To continue the work of Jesus and to express His will on earth, one must go beyond simply believing to ACTING on the authority Christ has given us.

## OUR AUTHORITY IN CHRIST AS CHILDREN OF GOD

According to Jesus and the Bible, we have been given authority to carry out the purposes of God to advance His Kingdom, heal the sick, and defeat the works of Satan and the powers of darkness. The chief barriers and influences that hinder our experience of freedom are the power of sin in its various forms and our enemy, the devil. Because these powers are at work, the all-surpassing power of Christ is manifested through us as we, in faith, utilize the authority He's given us to expose, defeat, and reverse his influence. The devil seeks to take advantage of any area of weakness, sin, or brokenness.

The Scriptures, particularly the New Testament, reveal the pervasive influence of Satan and evil in the world, as a supernatural power that must be recognized and confronted as Christ taught (Luke 4:5-7; Ephesians 2:1-3; 6:10-18; 1 John 5:19, etc.). This is perhaps the most under-utilized and misunderstood ability that God has given every believer.

Until the Kingdom of God comes in its fullness, the power and influence of evil will prevail in every allowable situation unless it is confronted with the power God has made available through Christ's sacrifice and triumph on the cross. He has given us power and authority to continue His ministry and defeat the powers that oppose Him and oppress people.

While God is sovereign over all, He chooses to work through His people. This is the history of God's activity from Genesis to Revelation. Without a doubt He does wonderful and powerful acts apart from any human involvement. However, He has chosen to use us in His plan to extend His Kingdom and the message of salvation until He returns. Our part is a response to the commission He gave us and it is an act of obedience to carry it out. For this reason, it is necessary to utilize the authority Christ has given us (instead of only asking Him) to thwart the influences of evil, and to test, expose, and resolve those influences that may hinder the work of Christ.

To act on the authority of Christ IS the exercise of faith (Matthew 8:5-13). The authority of Christ can be utilized by every believer to:

1. To confer the Holy Spirit. (Acts 2:38; 8:19;10:44-48; 19:6;)

2. To build up one another. (2 Corinthians 10:8; 13:10)

3. To heal. (Matthew 10; Luke 9:1-6; 37-43)

4. To cast out demons. (Matthew 10:8)

5. To bind and loose. (Matthew 16:19; 18:18)

6. To forgive sins. (John 20:22-23)

7. To impart God's peace (Matthew 10:13).

8. To declare and enforce God's truth and will. (Matthew 4:1-11)

9. To invoke His power to intervene and to insure His will is done. (Acts 13:9-12)

## NEW TESTAMENT SCRIPTURES REFERRING TO THE AUTHORITY OF THE BELIEVER

*"He called His twelve disciples to Him and gave them authority to drive out evil spirits and to heal every disease and sickness."* **Matthew 10:1**

*"I will give you the keys of the Kingdom of heaven; whatever you bind on earth will be bound in heaven, and whatever you loose on earth will be loosed in heaven."* **Matthew 16:19**

*"Then Jesus came to them and said, All authority in heaven and on earth has been given to me. Therefore go and make disciples of all nations, baptizing them in the Name of the Father and of the Son and of the Holy Spirit, and teaching them to obey everything I have commanded you. And surely I am with you always, to the very end of the age."* **Matthew 28:18-20**

*"Then Jesus had called the Twelve together, He gave them power and authority to drive out all demons and to cure diseases, and He sent them out to preach the Kingdom of God and to heal the sick."* **Luke 9: 1-2**

*"After this the Lord appointed seventy-two others and sent them two by two ahead of him to every town and place where He was about to go. He told them, The harvest is plentiful,*

*but the workers are few. Ask the Lord of the harvest, therefore, to send out workers into His harvest field ... Heal the sick who are there and tell them, The Kingdom of God is near you ... The seventy-two returned with joy and said, Lord, even the demons submit to us in Your name."* **Luke 10: 1-2, 9, 17**

*"Jesus said, I have given you authority to trample on snakes and scorpions and to over-come all the power of the enemy; nothing will harm you."* **Luke 10:19**

*"But you will receive power when the Holy Spirit comes on you; and you will be My witnesses in Jerusalem, and in all Judea and Samaria, and to the ends of the earth."* **Acts 1:8**

*"His intent was that now, through the church, the manifold wisdom of God should be made known to the rulers and authorities in the heavenly realms."* **Ephesians 3:10**

*"I tell you the truth, anyone who has faith in Me will do what I have been doing. He will do even greater things than these, because I am going to the Father. And I will do whatever you ask in My name, so that the Son may bring glo-ry to the Father. You may ask Me for anything in My name, and I will do it."* **John 14:12-14**

# DECLARING AND ACCEPTING GOD'S TRUTH

**3**

The final foundational principle for this Field Guide is declaring and accepting God's truth in the following ways:

- To take thoughts captive and make them obedient to Christ.

- To verbally confess and declare God's truth and to renounce that which is false.

- By accepting God's truth, submitting to (obeying) it despite the feelings we may have.

- To know your identity and purpose as a child of God and citizen of His Kingdom.

- To know, live by, declare and assert God's truth, will, and purpose.

- To pray on all occasions with all kinds of prayers.

- To verbally recall and rely on His promises and deeds in the past.

- To test and discern what is from God and what is not from God.

- As a weapon to expose, address and defeat Satan's schemes and influences.

- To forgive and release those who have offended you, their sins and effects to God.

Jesus said, *"If you hold to My teaching, you are really My disciples. Then you will know the truth and the truth will set you free."* **John 8:32**

Knowing the truth that leads to freedom involves more than mere intellectual assent or adequate knowledge of the Bible. Many people believe and are saved but not all are experiencing the freedom Christ promises and secured for them at the cross because they do not know (accept, submit to, or act on) the truth (Hebrews 4:2) or have not renewed their minds (Romans 12:2) with the truth.

> Knowing the truth means acknowledging the truth about God _and_ the truth about ourselves – what we have done, what has been done to us, what we've experienced and how we feel.

Instead, many Christians try to battle for their mind and/or overcome sinful or destructive behaviors, negative thoughts and recurring feelings through self-effort, discipline, increased learning, and/or religious activity – going to church, reading the Bible, praying, worship, conferences, etc. (2 Timothy 3:7; John 5:39). The Scriptures remind us (Romans 12:2) that transformation comes not by more effort or religious activity, but by renewing one's mind and by walking in the power of the Holy Spirit (Galatians 5:16). We renew our minds with the truth when we not only hear the truth, but accept it, submit to it, and obey it <u>despite</u> any feelings we have to the contrary.

Others find themselves in a frustrating cloud of hopelessness when it comes to experiencing personal transformation and freedom. They remain caught in an ongoing cycle of sin, confess and sin again. This cycle includes confusion from conflicting thoughts and emotions that keep them from experiencing the love and freedom Christ promised.

To know the truth that results in freedom begins with accepting and agreeing with the truth that comes from God, despite one's feelings, perceptions, and experiences to the contrary. Knowing the truth means acknowledging the truth about God <u>and</u> the truth about ourselves – what we have done, what has been done to us, what we've experienced and how we feel.

Many who remain stuck in this cycle of sin, confess and sin again often ask God for forgiveness with little or no experience of freedom or resolution. The experience of freedom remains elusive because it is not tied to forgiveness. The truth is that they are and have been forgiven from the moment they confessed their sin. This is the promise and assurance of God's Word (1 John 1:9) and what we must accept despite any feelings that remain as a result.

Even though a person may continue to experience the unresolved *effects* of their sin or the sins committed against them, they are nevertheless forgiven. The issue may instead have to do with renouncing the effects or false beliefs that came about as a result of one's sins and the sins of others. Further complicating matters are the powerful feelings that reinforce these lies and false beliefs. Renouncing out loud is an audible act where one exchanges one's beliefs or feelings for what God says is true. See #11 *Taking Thoughts and Feelings Captive* in Section II.

Furthermore it is important to reject any potential opportunities or inroads that the enemy has taken through the opportunity that was provided by one's sin or through the sins of others. It is also necessary to forgive those who have hurt us and to recognize and resolve the resulting patterns of false beliefs, destructive behaviors, and the negative thoughts and feelings that are opposed to God's truth. See #11 *Taking Thoughts and Feelings Captive* in Section II.

Knowing, accepting, and submitting to the truth is the key to freedom from lies or other spiritual influences of evil. It is also a necessary part of renewing one's mind. Satan and the unseen powers of darkness seek to influence and captivate the mind by introducing thoughts or ideas that appeal to one's feelings and natural appetites, and one's legitimate human needs in order to deceive us in a direction away from God's truth, provision and will (Genesis 3; Matthew 4). In fact, Satan seeks to take ad-

vantage of any opening or area of weakness and vulnerability – sin, trauma, fear, lies we believe or feelings we
have about ourselves, or others, and the way we perceive
things to be. This includes lies about God, who He is, or
what He is like.

We can accept what's true despite our feelings when
we are willing to admit the truth and simply agree with
what God says (because He *is* Truth and cannot lie –
Hebrews 6:18), then declare the truth aloud, and audibly
renounce that which is untrue. See #11 *Taking Thoughts
and Feelings Captive* in Section II. This kind of obedience
is only possible through the empowerment of God's Holy
Spirit as one relies on and requests His help, counsel, and
understanding.

## TEST EVERYTHING!

While we must take personal responsibility for our
own desires and behavior (James 1:14,15), we must also
realize there may be a spiritual influence of evil that is
influencing us and/or seeking to take advantage of us
and is holding us captive to our desires, thoughts, and
behaviors.

If an individual is unable to exercise their will or have
enough self-discipline to obey Jesus, walk in the Spirit
and increasingly manifest the fruit of His Holy Spirit, it
is quite likely that such an individual is in some form of
bondage from which they need to be set free. It is important to, *"Test everything, hold on to what is good; and avoid*

every kind evil." **1 Thessalonians 5:21-22** And, *"Test the spirits to see if they are from God"* **1 John 4:1** so that we do not continue to persist in a futile attempt to overcome our problems, sin, or circumstances without the power of God and the freedom to do so. It is wise to acknowledge the possibility of unresolved spiritual or psychological problems that may be at the root of one's bondage and lack of freedom. This is an essential part in the process of one's freedom and healing and should be considered a *routine test.* Once we test, expose, and discern potential spiritual influences of evil and/or other unresolved issues at the root of a person's problem and resolve them, we are free to exercise discipline, self-control, and crucify the flesh as we are empowered by the Holy Spirit to live in obedience and pursue freedom. See #19 *Freeing Those Who Are Oppressed* in Section III.

# SECTION II

THE NATURE AND
PRACTICE OF BIBLICAL
AND EFFECTIVE PRAYER

# 4

# A GENERAL PATTERN OF BIBLICAL PRAYER

## USE AND SETTING FOR APPLICATION

A guide for implementing some principles, language, and grammar of biblical prayer to utilize in our approach to prayer.

## PURPOSE AND DESCRIPTION

To increase our understanding and practice of the way Jesus and others in Scripture prayed. This a general pattern that typifies the nature of the Lord's Prayer and many other prayers represented throughout the Bible.

## APPLICATION

**1. Opening Address to God**

- Acknowledging who He is

- Reflects His character in a manner consistent with His acts of faithfulness

**2. Declaration, Assertion or Reconciliation**

- Regarding God's nature, promises, acts and will

- Moves from a rehearsal or declaration of what He has said, done, and wills to do, *therefore, now let it be so*. From word to life. From proclamation to fulfillment. Example of suggested vocabulary

  **TO GOD:** *Lord, You have said...* (verbalize and

declare God's Word, His promises, etc.*) and here's my situation...* (tell Him what's going on, what you need or the circumstances you are in) *so let it be as You have said."* (See example in 2 Chronicles 20:5-12)

**TO POWERS OF DARKNESS:** *Because God says... now let it be so according to His will.*

*It is written...*(state God's Word and promises as a command to be obeyed). Then give the command to obey: *therefore, we tell you Satan, in Jesus' Name...*(see Matthew 4:11-10)

*We agree according to God's Word...*(verbalize and declare God's Word, His promises, etc.) and *together claim...*(state your specific need, request in accordance with God's Word and will), *"Lord, because You have said or promised these things we now receive them for Your glory and according to our need" and together we forbid all that is opposed, in Christ's Name.*

### 3. Request, Petition, Claim or Appeal

- From a simple request to a bold claim on God's promises; the appropriation of something you have been rightfully given, have, or were promised.

- *Here's my situation...this is what you have promised...now let it be so according to Your will* (Genesis 32).

---

- *Because it is written…In Jesus' Name I (we) command any influence opposed to God's will, purpose or promise to leave and remove any hold or effect on _____ (Matthew 4:1:11)*

- An appeal or request based on who God is, His nature, promises, acts of power and demonstrations of faithfulness; how He has represented Himself and what He has said.

- An appeal or request with the honest and often preceding expressions of emotions expressed in words, feelings, and actions (Psalms, Jesus in Gethsemane)

- Making or presenting a case by appealing to reason, precedence, God's mercy, character, reputation, justice, etc. A judicial approach.

# EXAMPLES AND APPLICATIONS OF PRAYER

## TO ALMIGHTY GOD

## TO POWERS OF DARKNESS

### DECLARATION, APPEAL OR REQUEST

### ASSERTION OF AUTHORITY

**WHAT TO DO:**
Verbally state, speak out, declare, announce (like an edict from a king) what God said, promised, desires and wills; or making an appeal/request based on these things.

**WHAT TO DO:**
Audibly state the terms, rules, or truth as something to be obeyed and enforced by verbally declaring, appropriating or claiming what God wants, desires, wills, or promises. In Jesus' Name give orders to the demonic, sickness, etc.

### DECLARATION

*We honor You, Lord Jesus, and worship You as Lord of all. We invite Your presence and gather in Your Name. Together we assert Your Lordship, dominion and victory over every power and influence that has set its will against this place, God's purpose and those gathered here.*

*We (I) give You our thoughts, emotions and our will and ask You to align them with Your Truth and free us (me) to understand and hear Your voice.*

*We welcome and extend Christ's protection over every part of our being and over those we love and all that God has entrusted to us.*

### ASSERTION

*In Jesus' Name we command all that is opposed to the Lord Jesus Christ and to His purpose, to leave now. We send you to Christ for His judgment and determination. We command that you remove all of your influence and effects. We claim this place for the presence and purpose of Jesus Christ.*

*In Jesus' Name we (I) submit and secure our (my) vulnerable areas to Christ and forbid the evil one from influencing or affecting any part of our (my) mind, body or emotions.*

*And, we forbid any form of retaliation by the enemy against us or those we love, In Jesus' Name, Amen*

| TO ALMIGHTY GOD | TO POWERS OF DARKNESS |
|---|---|
| **DECLARATION, APPEAL OR REQUEST** | **ASSERTION OF AUTHORITY** |

## APPEAL

*Lord, You promised to guide us into all truth and to grant us whatever we ask and agree on in Your Name. We gratefully appropriate the mind of Christ and the Holy Spirit we've been given to know and do the Father's will.*

## ASSERTION

*So, In Jesus' Name, we forbid and banish all that opposes God's truth and the counsel of the Holy Spirit and we claim the mind of Christ and the counsel of the Spirit for we have the mind of Christ (1 Corinthians 2:16) and how much more will He give the Holy Spirit to those who ask?*

## REQUEST

*We seek Your counsel and ask You to show us what to pray about and what to do...our eyes are on You, Lord (2 Chronicles 20:12).*

Share and test thoughts, images or feelings that come to mind without sorting them out and pray about them seeking God's counsel and will.

*Because Your Word says ...*

*We ask ...*

## ASSERTION

*And, in Jesus' Name we command all that God has willed for us to know and pray about to be subject to His counsel and to come into the light of His truth. We forbid you enemy of God from hindering our communion with God and with one another through the Holy Spirit.*

*Therefore, together we (assert, forbid, claim, command) ...*

*And in Jesus' Name we ...*

**Additional verbs you can use in praying with authority:** announce, assert, banish, bind, claim, come against, come out, come, command, cut off sever, declare, demand, demolish, destroy, divide, expose, forbid, free, give back, go, hand over, inflict, leave, let go, loose, overthrow, proclaim, pronounce, reject, renounce, require, reverse, say you will be (blind, unable to see, mute, etc.), say, seize, send, separate, silence, speak to, strike, strip (of power and ability), subject, take back, take captive, tell you, we (I) hand you over.

# 5

# A CHECKLIST FOR EFFECTIVE PRAYER

## USE AND SETTING FOR APPLICATION

To be used in personal or corporate prayer and fasting.

## PURPOSE AND DESCRIPTION

This checklist provides a systematic and sequential approach that includes key components of effective biblical prayer utilizing God's Word, Christ's authority, and the counsel of the Holy Spirit. It is intended for individuals or groups who want to diligently contend for God's purpose and will to prevail and to thwart the influences that oppose it. This is a helpful tool for those who are intent and determined to see transformation in the lives of those they love or in regard to the things they care about.

## APPLICATION

✓ **What Does God Want?**

- Ask the Holy Spirit to guide you in searching for God's promises and various Scripture passages related to your particular situation.

- Write or type and print them out (index cards work great too). Your purpose here is to identify and become familiar with what God has promised you, what He wills and desires in regard to your situation and the matters you are praying about.

- The foundation for faith is God's Word and His faithfulness in who He is and in what He's done (Psalm 138:2; 2 Corinthians 1:20; Hebrews 6:18).

## ✓ Address God Personally and Directly

- Invite God's presence and be consciously aware that He is present just like He promised (John 14:17).

- Audibly and authoritatively forbid and banish any influence or presence of the evil one e.g., *If there is any influence present that is opposed to my fellowship and communion with the Lord Jesus Christ, I now command you in Jesus' Name to leave and go to the feet of Christ to be judged.* (Matthew 4:10)

- Begin speaking to Jesus in an audible and normal conversational tone of voice.

- Talk to Him in a personal and familiar manner by acknowledging who He is and thanking Him for what He's done.

- Use various names or characteristics of God that are consistent with His Word, His nature, and the nature of your particular need.

- Affirm and declare His Lordship and dominion. Let this be a time of worship, praise and adoration.

### ✓ Listen

- Verbally submit your mind, will, and emotions to Christ's control.

- Ask or claim the *mind of Christ* that He's given you and in Jesus' Name forbid any influence or distraction that would keep you from communing with Jesus through the Holy Spirit.

- Spend some time listening or being silent in His presence and simply write down or journal the thoughts, impressions, or images you are having.

- Instead of trying to think in advance about what you want to say, simply verbalize and pray about those things that come to mind.

- Evaluate or *test* the things that come to mind in light of God's Word to measure their consistency with His truth.

### ✓ Declare God's Truth and Promises

- In contrast to making a request or pleading, begin to declare aloud what God has promised and said in His Word.

- Instead of just quoting His words and promises it is important to *assert* them by declaring them as His absolute truth and the expression of His Sovereign will. For example:

- *Sovereign Lord, as You have promised* (Luke 2:29)
  *O Lord, You have said ...* (Exodus 33:12-23)
  (Genesis 32:9-12)

## ✔ Use Christ's Authority

- To forbid and expel any potential influence of evil that may be involved in your particular situation or that is opposing the will or promises of God in regard to your request

- Speak audibly and directly to any suspected evil spiritual influence giving clear, specific, directed and firm commands that represent God's will, promises, and truth. For example:

- *"It is written ... away from me Satan!"* **Matthew 4:1-11**

- *"In the name of Jesus Christ I command you ... "* **Acts 16:16-18**

## ✔ Declare and Recall What God Has Done

- Recall and audibly declare the things God has done – things He's done in the past as recorded in His Word and/or those things you've experienced in your personal life and have witnessed in the lives of others as evidence of His faithfulness.

- Declare them as an act of worship, an expression of faith, and an acknowledgement of His faithfulness in *making your case* (Psalm 105; Acts 4:24- 31)

### ✓ Build Your Case and Make Your Request

Ask, petition and appeal to God with your request in keeping with what He's said, done, and according to who He is and what He desires (His will).

Give your reasons for why God should grant your request by appealing to His Word, His promises, His nature (who He is), and His faithfulness expressed in what He's done.

With complete honesty, verbalize your true feelings to Him about your requests, desires, frustrations and fears. (Genesis 32:11; 2 Chronicles 20; Isaiah 38:1-4; Mark 14:34)

### ✓ Gather With Others

The context for most of the passages of Scripture in regard to prayer indicate the significance of corporate prayer and the resulting effectiveness of praying together. So, if your efforts in praying individually have not yielded the fruit of those things that you are praying for in accordance with God's will (the things He wants, promises, & wills), then try gathering with two or more to pray and contend (wrestle, battle) with you in regard to your situation. This, **along with using the authority Christ** has given you are the two most under-utilized and most effective tools God has given us to accomplish His purpose in prayer. (Matthew 18:19-20)

At times it may also be important to include a person who is a designated authority, either by nature of their position, or because of their role in God's economy – a pastor of a church, a leader of a particular ministry; head of a household, etc. There may be occasions where it's important to have a male authority figure, leader, or husband involved. This, of course, has nothing to do with gender equality and does not minimize the same authority that God has given to all believers. It may, however, make a difference in that Satan recognizes and seemingly responds to a representative male authority figure in circumstances where he does not seem to be responding to a female. The reason for this may have to do with the structure of authority God had originally established and the structure to which the Kingdom of Satan is still bound and subject to. In these matters we've observed that Satan is extremely legalistic in regard to the law, rules, and the semantics of how they are understood and communicated. Therefore, we must be clear and direct in our dealings with him and utilize the means of authority God has given and established. One example where this seems to make a significant difference is in the marriage covenant where the male is not fulfilling his role in being God's representative spiritual authority and in providing a covering for his household. In households where there is the absence of male representational

authority one can, in times of need, utilize the provision
God has provided through other trustworthy brothers in
the Body of Christ.

## ✓ Fasting and Prayer

- Jesus assumed that we would fast. *"When you fast
. . ."* **Matthew 6:17**

- Fasting is getting serious and purposeful about
getting God's way in your particular situation;
for what we sacrifice in the natural, we gain in
the spiritual. It is an intentional prioritization
of spiritual and eternal matters placed above our
natural desires, human appetites, and the cares
or concerns of this world. The process can develop from initial discipline to regularity and freedom as it becomes part of your life's rhythm and
schedule. It provides us with the opportunity to
engage with Jesus in the *real world* – the one that
is eternal and spiritual.

- Use the time gained from what you are fasting
from (food, television) to pray and contend.

- Ask others to pray for your strength and protection so you can focus on the matter at hand.

## ✓ Watch, Wait and Record

- In most cases the prayers of the Bible record some
kind of response to the individual's prayer. It is

most often a direct answer or recognizable action or indication of change.

- So, be watchful and look forward to what God will do and be mindful of the *way* He responds. Keep a written journal or record of progress and results. This will encourage you to remain diligent and expectant. Your journal will be important for being able to recall what God has done. This gives you an opportunity for praise and inspires the kind of faith you may need for things you face in the future.

- Be expectant, but not in the sense of how you think it might or should turn out. However, you can always be expectant of God's willingness to answer and act in His way!

## ✓ Be Alert!

- Always be aware that prayer is a battle and is a powerful instrument for affecting change. It will provoke and initiate activity in the spiritual realm.

- It must be emphasized that it is equally important to regularly utilize the authority you have been given in Christ to forbid and confront influences of evil as they seek to hinder and effect times of prayer, Bible study, those who are praying and the things being prayed for.

# 6

# PRAYING TOGETHER

## USE AND SETTING FOR APPLICATION

For corporate gatherings of prayer where two or more are gathered in Christ's Name.

## PURPOSE AND DESCRIPTION

A step-by-step guide to facilitate the effectiveness of corporate prayer gatherings and intercession. To insure that the focus is on the person of Christ who is present through His Spirit when we gather (Matthew 18:19-20) and that we rely on Him to lead and counsel us in prayer and corporate discernment as we listen to Him and interact with Him and those who are gathered as His body.

## APPLICATION

**Remember why you are gathering to pray:**

- To meet with God and to know Jesus.

- To affect change – to get God's way– *"Thy Kingdom come, Thy will be done."* **Matthew 6:10**

**To keep in mind while you gather:**

- The Lord Jesus Christ is present with us through His Holy Spirit so we can pray and respond accordingly. Purposefully and intentionally rely on Him.

- Be attentive to Him and how He may be leading

and guiding us individually and corporately as a group.

- Prayer is a spiritual battle and we are called to be alert before during and after to recognize, test, and resolve influences of evil that attempt to hinder our unity and God's purpose as we gather.

**What to do when you gather.**

- Environment First. See *#15 Environment First* in Section III

- Submit, Resist, Exchange

  - Submit to God  (Romans 12:1)

  - Choose to, and audibly declare your dependence on God by offering yourself as a vessel of His love, presence, and power by asking Him to fill empower and counsel you with His Holy Spirit.

  - Resist the devil (James 4:7, Ephesians 6:10-18)

  - Always use the authority Christ has given you to verbally and audibly speak to any and all spiritual influences or beings by commanding them in Jesus' Name to be bound, remain bound, not interfere, and especially to leave with all or any effects of their presence on or in the place you are gathered.

- Exchange (Isaiah 40:31)

- The idea of an exchange is conveyed in the promise of strength for those who *wait* upon the Lord. Here is the notion of dependence on the Lord and His strength (Ephesians 6:18). One can do so by audibly *exchanging* or trading one's own strength or weakness in return for the Lord's strength and power, one's fear for Jesus' peace. His spirit of power and of a sound mind (2 Timothy 1:7).

- Welcome God's presence with an invitation of invocation and an act of worship.

- Look to Jesus and ask the Holy Spirit to guide you individually and corporately into all truth and for His counsel and empowerment

**Respond in Obedience:**

By sharing what comes to mind in order to be tested. If there are those present who may be reluctant to share or if those gathered want to aim for greater objectivity, have participants write the things that come to mind in prayer onto 3x5 cards. They can be handed in, read, and tested. *Test everything* via process of corporate discernment. Communicate with those in authority and submit what you have corporately discerned to them. Do so in humility by sharing and submitting it for them to test and discern. Avoid statements like, "This is what the Lord is saying ... " or "This is what we have discerned from the Lord so here is what needs to happen." etc. If the matter is something they are responsible for deciding or doing, wait for them to have time to do so. While waiting, it is important to contend for and cover them, including coming against any works of the enemy that would try to affect your leaders and those in authority. Remember your battle is not against them but for them and primarily for the Lord's will to be done.

**Utilize God's Word and Christ's Authority:**

- As the absolute expression of His sovereign will – insist on it and enforce it (like a police officer or soldier on behalf of the authority they represent).

- As the basis of agreement and foundation of unity (John 17:21-23).

- By declaring it in agreement <u>for</u> the things God wants and wills, *It is written ... Therefore, let it be so.* (Matthew 4:1-11; Luke 4:1-13).

- By expressing it as a command to be obeyed against anything that seeks to oppose it, *In Jesus' Name, it is written ... therefore, you must ...*

# SAMPLE SCRIPTURES TO USE IN PRAYER

| PRAYING (CONTENDING) FOR | PRAYING (CONTENDING) AGAINST |
| --- | --- |
| **Truth** *John 8:32,15:26* | **Lies** *John 8:44b* |
| **Peace** *John 14:27* | **Anxiety** *Philippians 4:6-7* |
| **Clarity of Mind** *1 Corinthians 2:16* | **Clarity of Mind** *1 Corinthians 2:16* |
| **Revelation** *Ephesians 1:17* | **Fear** *2 Timothy 1:7* |
| **Freedom** *Galatians 5:1* | **Influences of the enemy** *Mark 8:33; Acts 13:11; 16:18* |
| **Leading of the Holy Spirit** *John 16:13-15* | **Presence of the enemy** *Matthew 4:1-11; Mark 8:33* |

# SAMPLE LANGUAGE TO USE IN PRAYER

| | |
| --- | --- |
| It is written...(declare the truth by stating Scripture)... therefore, let it be so. | Therefore, in Jesus' Name ... |
| | Satan, we command you to ... |
| According to God's will, we claim ... | In Jesus' Name, we expose ... |
| According to God's Word, we agree for ... | In Jesus' Name, we forbid ... |
| | In Jesus' Name, we reject ... |
| According to the word of God, we declare ... | In Jesus' Name, we come against ... |

### Record/Journal

Have someone serve as a designated recorder to journal those things that seem significant to keep praying about; that need further discernment; or matters that should be passed on to those in leadership.

### To Conclude:

Cover and seal each participant before and after prayer ministry to insure the well-being of those involved and the place of your meeting against any retribution from the enemy.

### Example:

*I assert the power and authority of the Lord Jesus Christ over this place and over each person here to cover and seal every part of their being. In Jesus' Name, I forbid any form of retaliation or harm and now command all influences opposed to Jesus to be bound and subject to Christ now. I cancel all your schemes and effects and send you now to Jesus for judgment. Leave now in Jesus' Name.*

# 7

# CONTRASTING INTERCESSION, AUTHORITY AND INTERACTIVE PRAYER

## USE AND SETTING FOR APPLICATION

To provide a visual and practical illustration to show the difference between prayer that is intercessory in nature (asking God and praying *for* things); and statements or declarations of Christ's authority, and prayer that is a three-way interactive conversation between God, those with whom or for whom you are praying.

## PURPOSE AND DESCRIPTION

To broaden our understanding of what it means to pray with all kinds of prayers, to take up the shield of faith, and to utilize the sword of the Spirit which *is* the Word of God for the purpose of effective prayer that yields biblical fruit, gets God's way, and insures that His will is done.

## APPLICATION

In every occasion of personal or corporate prayer.

> *"And pray in the Spirit on all occasions with all kinds of prayers and requests. With this in*

*mind, be alert and always keep on praying for*
*all the saints."*
**Ephesians 6:18, I Thessalonians 5:17**

Most of us are comfortable with intercession, yet we often stop short when it comes to using the authority Christ has given us in prayer or to expose and resolve influences of evil. We must go beyond simply believing to acting on the authority given to us by Jesus if we want to affect change that results in transformation. We must also recognize that using our authority in Christ is an act of faith that honors Jesus' sacrifice and is the catalyst for the advancement of His Kingdom and for the defeat of Satan and the powers of darkness. (Luke 11:20) If we want to truly emulate Christ then we will do what He did and what He taught His disciples to do.

An interactive and corporate approach to prayer includes asking God, who is present by His Spirit, to lead and counsel us as we learn to listen and respond to His leading and that which He reveals. It is what the Old Testament often refers to as *inquiring of the Lord* where individuals or groups gather to seek the Lord and His counsel (2 Chronicles 20:1-15). Using intercession, authority and interactive prayer together is a discipline that takes time and practice. With Jesus as a model and the various prayers and interventions in the Bible, we can use all kinds of prayers to more effectively advance God's will and purpose in a variety of situations.

| PRAYER | COMMAND | COUNSEL |
|---|---|---|
| *TO GOD* | *FOR GOD* | *WITH GOD* |
| In the Spirit Ephesians 6:18 | In Jesus' Name As an ambassador of Christ Acts 3:6,7; 16:18 | Through the counsel of the Holy Spirit John 14:26;16:13-14 |
| With all kinds of requests and prayers Ephesians 6:18; I Timothy 2:1 | Declaring God's truth (Mt. 4:1-10) Asserting His Will (I Sam. 17; Acts 2:14-39; 4:10-12) | Inquiring of the Lord Acts 1:12-26; I Chronicles. 14:8-15:15 |
| | Speaking directly to demonic influences & sickness (Acts 3:6; 16:18) | In dialog with one another Mark 8:22-26; Acts 1:14-26 |
| Asking, calling out, and appealing to God according to His Word and will. John 17; Acts 4:24-31 | Commanding, declaring, binding, loosing, casting out, renouncing, forbidding, canceling, forgiving, imparting | Asking Jesus, The Holy Spirit to counsel, reveal, and guide us into truth John 14-16 |
| | | Listening & responding to His lead; to one another |
| Lord Jesus, we ask ... because You said ... (promises, Word) | In Jesus' Name, we command ... In Jesus' Name, we declare and/or assert ... | Spirit of God, we ask that You will counsel and reveal ... show us ... |

# 8

# ADDRESSING POTENTIAL ENVIRONMENTAL INFLUENCES OF EVIL

## USE AND SETTING FOR APPLICATION

Prior to or during gatherings for worship, prayer, ministry or outreach or as otherwise discerned or needed.

## PURPOSE AND DESCRIPTION

The following application is an example of engaging in intercessory prayer and declaring the truth in agreement, using the authority Christ has given you in your home, classroom, church, workplace or other environments where you desire the presence and will of God. Notice the shift between intercession and authority, the nature and tone of the grammar as well as the verbs used.

## APPLICATION

Declare the following aloud and in faith:

*We (I) assert the victory and Lordship of Jesus Christ, the Son of God, over this (home, room, place) and over each person who is (or will be) gathered (or lives) here. In the name of Christ, we now forbid and cut off all influences of Satan and the unseen powers of darkness. In Jesus' Name you are bound and silenced. We cancel all of your schemes and your effects and send you to Jesus for judgment. Leave now, in Jesus' Name.*

*Lord Jesus, we honor You and worship You as Lord of*

*all. We ask You to come and fill this place with Your holy presence. Spirit of God, we welcome You here among us and ask that Your presence of Light would remain with us, exposing and expelling darkness in order to fulfill Your purpose here and in the lives of those gathered. We ask You, Spirit of God, to guide us into all truth just as You promised. Lead and empower us in prayer. Counsel us and speak through us. Empower us to do Your will and release Your resources for the building up of Your Body, the Church, in Jesus' Name, Amen.*

# 9

# ADDRESSING POTENTIAL PERSONAL INFLUENCES THAT AFFECT OTHERS

## USE AND SETTING FOR APPLICATION

For family members, children, loved ones, those you are interceding for in regard to salvation, protection, and for those who have wandered from Christ.

## PURPOSE AND DESCRIPTION

To expose and address potential influences of evil that may be affecting people that we care about and are praying for in regard to freedom, healing, salvation, and protection. The following is an example of prayer and utilizing the truth along with the authority of Christ in regard to another person or persons.

## APPLICATION

**Declare aloud and in faith:**

*In Jesus' Name, we assert the victory and Lordship of Christ over _____. Because she/he is made in the image of God and is His very own creation, we claim her/his mind, body, and soul for the Lord Jesus Christ and the fulfillment of His purpose in and through her/his life. In Jesus' Name we command you Satan to remove all of your influences from her/his life and we cancel all of your effects, as well as your plans and purposes for her/him. We command that you remove the blinding effects of your influence in order that she/he may see the light and glory of Christ who is the image of God. We command all of your lies to come into the light of God's truth. Because God wills her/his freedom and desires that all people come to the knowledge of His truth, we command you to loose her/him to know God, live for Him, and to experience the love and freedom of Christ. In Christ's Name we extend God's protective covering over her/him and her/him mind to shield her/him from all harm and every form of deception.*

*Lord Jesus, we honor and worship you as Lord of all. Therefore we ask You now to draw _____ to Yourself according to Your desire, will and purpose. We ask that You send Your Holy Spirit to draw her/him to Yourself. We ask for a revelation of Jesus Christ to her/his mind and heart. May she/he recognize Your love and presence, and listen to Your voice. Keep her/him from listening to the evil one and to the lies she/he has heard or believed. Surround her/him with Your Light and protect her/him from the evil one. We ask that You would shield her/him with Your power and free her/him to fulfill the purpose for which You created her/him. We give her/him to You and trust in Your unfailing love. In Jesus' Name, Amen.*

# 10

# CORPORATE EXPRESSIONS OF AUTHORITY AND PRAYER

## USE AND SETTING FOR APPLICATION

In corporate gatherings for prayer prior to and/or during gatherings for worship, ministry and outreach; for intercession in regard to a city, community, neighborhood or a geographical area where there is a corporate effort to advance God's Kingdom.

## PURPOSE AND DESCRIPTION

The following is an example of utilizing Christ's authority when two or more are gathered (Matthew 18:18-20) in Jesus' Name to agree together for the purposes of God to prevail and to corporately come against the Kingdom of darkness in regard to your church, city, or mission outreach and for the well-being and protection of those in leadership and positions of authority. Again, please notice the shift in grammar between intercession and authority.

## APPLICATION

**Declare the following aloud and in faith:**

*In the name of Jesus Christ the resurrected Son of God, we come against you, Satan, and all the unseen powers of darkness. We assert the victory and Lordship of Jesus Christ over every plan and work of evil that is purposed against _____ and forbid you*

---

*from carrying them out. In Christ's Name we destroy your works, cancel your effects and forbid you from hindering or affecting the plans and purposes of God or the well-being of His people. We expose every scheme and instrument of evil and command every hidden thing to come into the light of Christ and become subject to Him and His truth. Together we claim the fulfillment of God's purpose in and through _____ . We assert His protective covering over every part of his/her being.*

*Lord Jesus, we honor You as Lord of all. Together we agree, "Your Kingdom come now, right here and Your will be done here and now on earth, in this place, and in our lives, as it is in heaven." Deliver him/her from the evil one. Empower him/her with Your Spirit, enable him/her to hear Your voice and do Your will in order that he/she may fulfill Your purpose, in Jesus' Name, Amen.*

# 11

# TAKING THOUGHTS AND FEELINGS CAPTIVE TO MAKE THEM OBEDIENT TO CHRIST

## USE AND SETTING FOR APPLICATION

To be used for personal discipleship to deal with lies, negative thoughts and emotions, or a part of your ministry to help others.

## PURPOSE AND DESCRIPTION

To discern between what is human thinking, feelings, satanic influence, and the truth that comes from God. While it is important for an individual to accept and declare the truth despite how they feel, this is not to suggest that one should ignore or minimize his or her feelings. Rather it is to acknowledge that one's feelings, while real, may not be an accurate gauge of what is true from God's perspective. Our feelings are like a compass needle that always points to *magnetic* north – a large magnetic field somewhat east of the North Pole. It's in a northerly direction but it's not an accurate guide for getting to True North. In fact, if you were to simply follow the direction represented by the compass needle for any significant distance, you may be far enough off course to miss your destination entirely.

*While our feelings represent how we feel, we know they don't always represent the truth.* If we continue to be guided by our feelings they will inevitably lead us in the wrong direction. Like the compass needle, they can be pulled in a direction away from or just slightly off course from what is true. God's Word, like True North, the North Pole, and the North Star, is a constant we can rely on and an accurate direction by which we can set our course and clear up the confusion that comes from the magnetic pull of our emotions and the unresolved feelings resulting from our collective experiences and our past.

Feelings are given to us by God. Every individual was given the same set of emotions when God created us. As such our feelings are important and should not be ignored or suppressed. They should be talked about and allowed expression, as they represent the truth about how one feels. However they do not always represent the truth that is from God or the way things are. It is therefore helpful and important to allow people to freely admit their honest feelings to God and to experience them (Psalm 106).

## APPLICATION

Perhaps the best biblical illustration and example of how to take thoughts and feelings captive to make them obedient is seen in Jesus response to temptation in the desert (Matthew 4:1-11) and during His emotional battle in the Garden of Gethsemane (Matthew 26:36-45). The following is a practical break down of this important act of obedience:

**Begin with a verbal prayer (aloud) of surrender to Jesus:**

*Lord Jesus, I submit my mind, thoughts and feelings to Your control so I can know Your truth and live in the freedom You will for me. I claim the mind of Christ You have given me and in Jesus' Name, I suspend, forbid and cancel all influences and effects of Satan and all that is opposed to Christ and His truth and command them to go to the feet of Christ to be judged right now. Holy Spirit, I exchange my thoughts and feelings for Your truth, counsel, and peace so I can remain in Your love and live in Your light. I ask for and claim the truth You promised in Jesus' Name.*

**Admit, Accept and Declare the Truth:**

- Admit and accept the truth *about how you feel* – admit *your truth* or feelings aloud and/or write them down.

- Declare (verbalize aloud) *God's truth* and accept that it is His truth.

- Admit and accept the truth about what you have experienced – how you were hurt and how it made you feel.

- Verbally admit (confess) any sins committed or omitted as the Holy Spirit reveals them **and** accept His forgiveness and truth despite how you feel because the truth is… (1 John 1:9, Romans

8:1, Hebrews 4:14-16, or other Scriptures that reveal God's truth in light of your feelings).

## Renouncing Lies and Unrighteous Effects

In regard to lies audibly say or repeat something like ... *In Jesus' Name, I renounce (reject) the lie that* _____ _____ *and I accept God's truth that*

*says* _____

In regard to things participated in, experienced, or associated with ... *In Jesus' Name, I renounce (cut off) all spiritual influences associated with* _____
*(sin committed or committed against them, acts of unrighteousness, sexual unions; traumatic experiences, forms of idolatry, evil influences through association with things or people, etc.).*

## Canceling the Effects of Unrighteousness and Evil

*And, in Jesus' Name, I (we) cancel all effects and influences that came about through, or as a result of (believing this lie, what I experienced, any opening given to the enemy, etc.), and send them away from me and to Christ for His judgment. Lord Jesus, I ask you to restore and protect every part of my/his/her being that has been affected .*

## Connect With Others in the Body of Christ to:

• Express thoughts/feelings to those who will listen, pray for you, and not judge.

- Ask for and receive prayer and personal ministry utilizing an interactive approach to prayer. See #7 *Contrasting Intercession, Authority and Interactive Prayer* in Section II. For more on how to identify and resolve negative behaviors, patterns of thinking, and emotions at their point of origin please see notes, resources, and training opportunities for "Leading Others To Freedom" at www.**Kingdom**Ministries**Intl**.org.

- Request and receive prayer from those who are willing to use God's Word and Christ's authority to contend for your covering (protection), engage in spiritual warfare on your behalf, and serve as a person in a committed relationship of accountability.

- To help you resolve root issues in your pursuit of freedom, healing, and sanctification.

- Who are gifted, called, and trained as professional counselors or behavioral practitioners to help you understand your feelings and learn to express them in productive and healthy ways.

- Assist you with professional medical and/or psychological services and/or an evaluation to diagnose and treat additional contributing factors.

OUTREACH

# SECTION III

KINGDOM EVANGELISM
AND OUTREACH

# BIBLICAL EVANGELISM

## USE AND SETTING FOR APPLICATION

For personal witness, evangelistic outreach, missions and anywhere one purposes to proclaim the Good News of the Kingdom of God in the manner Jesus, His Disciples, and the early church did.

## PURPOSE AND DESCRIPTION

To develop a biblical understanding and practice of evangelism based on the activity of Jesus, the disciples, and the New Testament church. This model is based on the example Jesus showed His followers. His specific instructions to His disciples and the seventy-two others were to:

Preach this message: The Kingdom of heaven is near.

Heal the sick.

Raise the dead.

Cleanse those with leprosy.

Cast out demons.

Furthermore, this is the same activity we observe the early believers being engaged in as they were empowered by the Holy Spirit to carry out Jesus' Great Commission locally and to the ends of the earth. To effectively proclaim the Good News of the Kingdom, we must go beyond a presentation of the gospel as something centered only on conversion and new birth. Above all, our foundation for evangelism must emphasize and include the confession of the **exclusive Lordship of Jesus Christ**, the one and only crucified and resurrected Son of God. This foundation must also be attended with the love and power of God that inspires faith and results in transformation. In order to effectively proclaim the Good News, we must first have a basic understanding of what Jesus meant by the Kingdom of God and then how to proclaim it.

## APPLICATION

The following sections and applications aim to provide practical tools and applications for evangelistic ministry and public outreach in the context of Jesus' message and ministry of the Kingdom of God.

### The meaning of GOSPEL

The word *gospel* is from an original New Testament word that refers to *Good News.* These terms are used interchangeably to mean the same thing. However, it's important to know where this New Testament Greek word came from and how it was used in the Bible and in the common language of the day. The following are a few summarized excerpts that help give us a clearer understanding of what Gospel or the Good News meant and means for us today as we go into all the world with the Good News to make disciples of all nations.

The word *gospel* was used to refer to an announcement or proclamation that contained a message of good news and brought relief, joy and hope for those who received it. For example, when a king would conquer a new territory there would be an announcement and/or a written proclamation (a *gospel*) to declare the good news of victory. It was a pronouncement that the land conquered is now under the newly established rule of the conquering king and his Kingdom.

It also can and did refer to the one who brings a *gospel* or good news; a messenger – one who brings or announces the gospel or good news – a message of victory or other political or personal announcement that causes joy. This variation of the word *gospel* is also where we get our word for evangelist.

When Jesus announces that the Kingdom of God is at hand, He is proclaiming a gospel. When He speaks, it is at the same time accomplished; He commands it and it is done.

Most of all, the word *gospel* is primarily used as a term to refer to a message of victory.

Perhaps most important is the significance of the word *gospel* as a proclamation or an announcement. A *gospel* was not simply information or a news report. *Rather, the proclamation of a gospel was a declaration that what was announced has come into being or was at the moment being initiated.* In other words, the announcement itself initiates and brings about its own fulfillment; what is spoken comes into being.

When Jesus announces that the Kingdom of God is at hand, He is proclaiming a *gospel. When He speaks, it is at the same time accomplished*; He commands it and it is done. So, not only is Jesus' announcement of the Kingdom of God a proclamation that a new reality is here or a new era has begun, it actually brings it about.[1]

This really is Good News! It helps us understand both the significance of the messenger and the message. With Jesus' arrival on the scene and His announcement of the Good News, salvation, freedom, and peace become a reality. When the Apostle Paul uses the word *gospel* he is not only referring to the content of his preaching but the power of God that attends it (1 Corinthians 2:1-5). His Spirit-empowered message had the effect *"to open their eyes and turn them from darkness to light, and from the power of Satan to God, so that ... they may receive forgiveness of sins and a place among those who are sanctified by faith ... "* **Acts 26:18;** to affect healing, freedom from demonic oppression, and dismantle the work of Satan and his attempts to interfere with the message, ministry, and mission of Christ (Acts 13:4-12; 16:16-18). In the same way we are to proclaim this gospel of the Good News of the Kingdom of God and the message about Jesus with power and effect (Acts 28:31). To do so creates faith, brings salvation, life, fulfillment of hope, and the awareness of judgment.

---

1    [4] Dictionary of New Testament Theology. Vol 1, Editor: Colin Brown

# 13

# SIGNS OF THE KINGDOM OF GOD

## USE AND SETTING FOR APPLICATION

A checklist of key indicators for those who are participating in and promoting the central elements of the Kingdom of God in life, ministry, and evangelism at home or abroad.

## PURPOSE & DESCRIPTION

To serve as a guide and increase our awareness of key elements, indicators, or signs that are part of what it means to proclaim Jesus' message of the Kingdom of God. Jesus and those who followed Him not only announced the good news of God's Kingdom, they were vessels of God's power, pointing to Jesus as the one and only true God. These *signs* also testified to their words and illustrated that what they spoke of was real.

## APPLICATION

*"As you go, preach this message: 'The Kingdom of heaven is near.' Heal the sick, raise the dead, cleanse those who have leprosy, drive out demons. Freely you have received, freely give."* **Matthew 10:7-8**

*"And these signs will accompany those who believe: In My name they will drive out demons; they will speak in new tongues; they will pick up snakes with their hands; and when they drink deadly poison, it will not hurt them at all; they will place their hands on sick people, and they will get well."* **Mark 16:17-20**

# SIGNS OF THE KINGDOM[1]

**Jesus in the midst of His people.**
*Matthew 18:20*

**Preaching the Gospel of the Kingdom.**
*Luke 4:18,19*

**Casting out demons.**
*Luke 11:20*

**Healing and nature miracles.**
*John 5, Mark 4:35-41*

**Conversion and new birth.**
*John 3:3*

**People manifesting the fruit of the Spirit.**
*Acts 2:42-47; Galatians 5:22-26*

**Suffering and persecution.**
*Matthew 10:17-23; John 15:20*

1   International Consultation on the Relationship Between Evangelism and Social Responsibility.  Lausanne Committee for World Evangelization. Grand Rapids, 1982. www.lausanne.org

# 14

# PRACTICAL GUIDELINES FOR PREACHING THE GOOD NEWS OF THE KINGDOM OF GOD

## USE AND SETTING FOR APPLICATION

For use in evangelistic efforts, mission outreach, or wherever one is purposed to carry out Jesus' commission to preach the Good News of the Kingdom and make disciples.

## PURPOSE AND DESCRIPTION

The following principles are intended to serve as a guide to help plan and conduct public evangelistic ministry and outreach. The guidelines given are consistent with the central signs of the Kingdom listed to the left and that are evident in the ministry of Jesus and the disciples.

## APPLICATION

Prior to evangelistic ministry or gatherings, gather together as God's people to pray, seek His counsel, build one another up as the Spirit of God leads you and to worship (Matthew 18:19-20).

Invite or invoke God's presence in the place you plan to gather and conduct your ministry and evangelistic outreach. Consecrate the place in which you are gathering and those who will gather. Secure the environment (area, territory) by setting it apart for Christ and His purpose. See #8 *Addressing Potential Environmental*

*Influences of Evil* in Section II.

Agree together in prayer for the things God has willed and desired in this setting and for the purpose of your gathering. Use #5 *Checklist for Effective Prayer* in Section II as a guide with promises and scriptures like 2 Peter 3:9; 1 Timothy 2:4; John 6:44; and Luke 15:4-7.

## PREACH THIS MESSAGE: THE KINGDOM OF GOD IS AT HAND

The message of the Kingdom is first and foremost a message about its King. As a critical part of your message and central to salvation is the declaration that Jesus Christ is Lord (Romans 10:9-10).

Declare "Jesus Christ is Lord" audibly and as a proclamation of His dominion and Lordship over all. This can be done in prayer, or as part of a testimony, a confession that is repeated, as a declaration during the preaching, Scripture reading, during an invitation, a Bible story, skit, or other media used to convey the Gospel message (Acts 2:21-24; 36-39).

Declare that there is salvation through no one else (Acts 4:12; Ephesians. 2:8,9). Lovingly but directly challenge hearers to **turn away** (repent) from: other gods, sin, self, and **turn to** and follow Jesus Christ as Lord; that the only other alternative is to remain in bondage to the powers of darkness and Satan (2 Corinthians 4:4; Galatians 4:3, 8-9; Ephesians 2:1-2).

Then, in audible prayer and with Christ's authority, invite Jesus' presence and power to confirm the truth of your message. Ask the Father to draw them to Jesus through the power of His Holy Spirit. At the same time utilize Christ's authority to forbid any influence or power that would seek to hinder the knowledge of the truth or deceive those who are present; give a direct command to Satan, in Jesus' Name, to remove any blinding effects that would keep anyone from hearing, knowing and responding to the truth by their own free will (2 Corinthians 4:4).

**For example:**

*In Jesus' Name, I command any influence that opposes Christ and the knowledge of the truth to be silent and subject to the Lord Jesus Christ. I now command you to come into the light of Christ to be exposed in order that any form of bondage that has resulted from your influence be revealed to each individual who is or who has been affected. In Jesus' Name, I command you to remove any blinding effects or influence that would keep anyone from seeing the light and glory of Christ who is the image of God so they can know the truth, see and hear clearly, and make their own decision; and respond of their own free will. Amen.*

Invite those present to **respond** in the following way

- Those who would like to know and follow the Lord Jesus Christ; give their allegiance to Him; have a life of purpose and freedom with the promise of forgiveness and eternal life (Romans 10:9,10).

- Those who would like to receive prayer for healing.

- Those who would like to receive freedom from anything that is evil that harms them, oppresses them or stands in the way of God's purpose for their life and His promise of abundant life.[2]

- Prepare and initiate a plan to personally interact with and minister to those who respond:

- By calling them to meet those who are prepared to minister in a particular location.

- By some indication of a response – standing or raising of a hand. This is particularly useful when it is necessary or desired to minimize the transition and movement of those who respond. Ministry and personal interaction can take place in the gathering as those equipped to minister can move to them where they are.

---

2  A biblical approach to evangelism and ministry will necessarily include each of these invitations and call for a response on the response on the part of the hearers. Even the important and profound declaration of Christ's Lordship can initiate a response from the heart by those who are present (Acts 2:37). By contrast, offering an altar call only for the purpose of inviting others to accept Jesus into one's heart, while certainly worthwhile, is nevertheless an incomplete proclamation of the gospel by New Testament standards. Again, the signs that indicate the presence and activity of God's Kingdom as well as the specific and exclusive commission of Jesus that includes not only the verbal proclamation of the Good News; but the demonstration or reality of that proclamation in the ministry of healing the sick, raising the dead, cleansing those with leprosy, and casting out demons is the biblical norm and model to follow.

- Plan to have at least one other person to minister with you – one who ministers and the other who prays, contends, and covers both minister and respondent.

- If you are in a foreign country, plan to have enough interpreters who are ready and able to assist the number of those who are ministering.

- **ALWAYS** and **without exception** ask each person who responds one or both of these questions:

- Would you like to know and follow Jesus as Lord? What would you like Jesus to do for you?

# 15

# ENVIRONMENT FIRST

## USE AND SETTING FOR APPLICATION

For use in public settings for ministry and worship to first deal with any environmental opposition including forces of darkness that are purposed against the will of God and/or aimed to disrupt ministry before it takes place (Matthew 8:23-34).

## PURPOSE AND DESCRIPTION

This is an essential intervention for consecrating a place, a geographical area, building, meeting room or gathering.

## APPLICATION

Do this by preparing, setting apart (consecrating) the specific place where you are meeting, the time, and the people who will be gathered to God. Use the authority you have been given in Christ to declare something like the following:

*We (I) declare Jesus Christ as Lord of all and assert His dominion over the place we are gathered, over this time, for the purpose we are gathered, and over all those who are present. In Christ's Name, we now cut off and forbid all outside influences and interferences of Satan and the unseen powers of darkness. In Jesus' Name, you are bound and silenced. We cancel all your schemes and effects and forbid you from interfering or distorting the proclamation or understanding of the Gospel. In Jesus' Name we subject you to Christ's authority and will during this time and command you to go where He tells you.*

Following this declaration begin to worship, exalt and honor the name of Jesus proclaiming His Lordship, victory and truth. Invite His holy presence and light to fill the room or place you are meeting. Together in agreement, seek and ask for the presence and specific counsel of His Holy Spirit. Ask Him to lead you – to pray and bring to mind all He wants to do. Ask Him to express His gifts through you to glorify Jesus and minister in His name (1 Corinthians 14:26-33). As the Spirit of God directs you (this means it may not be necessary all the time!), anoint (mark as consecrated or set apart to the Lord) persons, places, things, with oil, in the name of Christ (James 5:14; Exodus 40:9; Leviticus 8:12).

### DECLARATION

Follow the Holy Spirit's leading and pray in agreement according to the Scriptures while using Christ's authority to declare aloud God's intentions and purposes. For example:

*We claim the minds and hearts of those gathered here for the Lord Jesus Christ and for the fulfillment of His purpose in their lives. We cancel every scheme and all effects of the evil one and command you, Satan, to suspend your blinding effects on their minds so that they may see the light of*

*the Gospel of the glory of Christ who is the image of God.*
*2 Corinthians 4:4.*

## PRAY UTILIZING GOD'S WORD

*Father, we ask that You will begin to draw men and women to Yourself by the Holy Spirit (John 6:44). We claim their hearts, minds and bodies for the Lord Jesus Christ, in order that they may fulfill the purpose for which You created them, and to know the truth that sets them free. We agree with Your word that says You desire that all people come to a knowledge of the truth (1 Timothy 2:4) and that none perish or live an eternal life apart from You (2 Peter 3:9). We pray that You will enable them to hear and respond to Your truth. We also pray that You will restrain the powers of darkness from interfering and keeping them from knowing life in Christ and the freedom that comes by knowing Jesus and His truth, in Jesus' Name, Amen.*

Audibly through teaching, preaching, drama, testimony, or in the manner, method, or media you feel led by Jesus to use, present the Gospel after discerning together His particular plan or strategy for your outreach. In your presentation and central to the message, declare that Jesus Christ is Lord, and, that there is salvation through no one else or by any other means (Acts 4:12 and Ephesians 2:8,9).

# 16

# LEADING OTHERS TO FOLLOW CHRIST AS LORD

## USE AND SETTING FOR APPLICATION

In settings for personal or public ministry where one desires to lead another person into a personal relationship with Christ in order to know Him and follow Him as disciple.

## PURPOSE AND DESCRIPTION

The following approach is intended to assist those who are leading one or more persons to make a commitment to follow Jesus Christ as Lord of their lives according to Romans 10:9-10. The purpose is to establish a foundation on Jesus' Lordship and to turn, separate from, or renounce allegiance to any other god or idol including oneself.

## APPLICATION

### Ask the Question

Ask them, "Would you like to know Jesus?" (Acts 2:37). Observe and listen carefully to their response. Be aware of the battle for the mind. Bring their questions or concerns to Jesus. Ask them if you could pray with them and talk to Jesus about their questions or concerns ("let's ask Jesus . . ."). Ask Jesus to reveal Himself and His truth to their minds. Use Jesus' authority to forbid the influences of lies or darkness (*In Jesus' Name, I forbid any influence opposed to Christ . . .).*

## Lead Them to Christ

Ask them, "Do you believe in your heart that God raised Jesus from the dead and that Jesus Christ is Lord? Have them verbally (aloud) personalize or repeat Romans 10:9-10, for example: *I believe in my heart that God raised Jesus Christ from the dead and now declare that Jesus Christ is Lord of all.[3] I accept Him and submit to Him as Lord of my life. I now renounce all the influences and works of Satan in my life and ask You Jesus to come and fill me with Your presence and empower me with Your Holy Spirit, so that I can live for You as a child of God and as a member of Your family in the Body of Christ.*

## Repentance and Renunciation

*Jesus, because I have declared You Lord of my life, I also renounce (disown) all the things I have looked to, relied upon, or believed, that are opposed to You and Your truth (2 Corinthians 4:3). Lord, please forgive me for all of the things I have said, done, or believed that were wrong in Your eyes and that have kept me from knowing Your love and truth. Lord, search my heart and reveal to my mind*

---

3    If an individual indicates that they do not know or is not sure whether or not God has in fact raised Jesus from the dead, ask them to agree with you in prayer to ask God Himself! Take this question and any others back to Jesus and ask the Holy Spirit to reveal truth to them. Don't try to give an answer or come up with one even as this most often proves unfruitful due the spiritual battle over their decision. As you do, remember to, "In Jesus' Name, expose and forbid any form of deception and command that all things be subject to the Source of all truth."

*the ways that are offensive to You so that I may walk in the way that leads to everlasting life (Psalm 139:24).* Wait and have them confess the things that come to mind as the Lord reveals them.

# 17

# BAPTIZING IN THE NAME OF THE FATHER, SON, AND HOLY SPIRIT

## USE AND SETTING FOR APPLICATION

For public confession and testimony of one's commitment to follow and serve the Lord Jesus Christ.

## PURPOSE AND DESCRIPTION

Baptism is the first commitment and act of obedience following one's confession of faith of Jesus Christ as Lord. It is a public declaration of faith in one exclusive Lord and Savior, the crucified and resurrected Son of God, Jesus Christ. It is also an act of rejecting and separating from allegiance to any other god, idol, religion, self-will, or person other than the Lord Jesus Christ. It is a significant spiritual event that can affect the degree of freedom one experiences from the power of sin and darkness.

## APPLICATION

Ask those who have confessed Jesus as Lord if they would like to follow Him in baptism as an act of obedience in the washing away of their sin, receiving the Holy Spirit, and entering a new life (Acts 2:38; 22:16; Romans 6:4; 1 Corinthians 12:13; Galatians 3:27).

If they are willing, baptize them "In the name of the Father, Son, and Holy Spirit."

Ask them if they would like to receive the empowerment and filling of the Holy Spirit to fulfill God's purpose, manifest the fruit of the Spirit – love, joy, peace, etc. (Galatians 5:22-25), and receive His gifts (Romans 12; I Corinthians 12-14) to build up His Body and minister in His Name.

If so, lay hands on them and ask the Father to fill (empower, anoint, wash, overwhelm) them with the Holy Spirit and to impart His spiritual gifts through them for the glory of God, and the fulfillment of His purpose. In addition, while laying your hands upon them and with the authority you have been given in Christ speak aloud, *"Receive the Holy Spirit, in the Name of Jesus Christ, Amen."* Allow some time to wait on God's Spirit to work. Interact with the person you're praying with to see how they are doing and find out what they are thinking and/or experiencing. Be sure to test and discern the things they share in prayer together to see if they have significance and to discover what the Lord may be revealing or doing.

If necessary, ask Jesus to reveal anything that would keep them from experiencing the work and ministry of the Holy Spirit. Be aware of the battle of the mind. Ask Jesus to reveal Himself and His truth to their minds. Also remember to consistently use Jesus' authority to forbid the influences of lies or darkness that would seek to interfere or deceive.

# 18

# PRAYING FOR THOSE WHO ARE SICK

## USE AND SETTING FOR APPLICATION

The example given below is primarily intended for use in evangelistic settings to minister to those who are sick and desire Jesus to heal them. In this setting you will find that God often heals in order to inspire faith in Christ for those who receive prayer and/or are healed.

## PURPOSE AND DESCRIPTION

The purpose for this particular approach is rooted in Jesus' model of ministering to the sick. It begins with the same questions Jesus asked people prior to his authoritative interventions and their resulting healing.

## APPLICATION

Ask those who are sick if they would like to receive prayer for healing. Do not promise them healing or tell them they are healed. Instead, let them tell you. They will know and can testify to what has happened or to what has not. In fact, it is important to encourage prayer recipients to be honest with you regarding their progress, what they are experiencing and/or feeling. This will only help you be more effective in ministering to them and in recognizing how God may be leading you and directing the focus of your prayer.

Begin by asking the person you are praying for some

of the same questions Jesus asked, for example:

- "Do you want to get well?" (John 5:5-7). If the answer is *yes* ask them:

- "What (specifically) would you like God to do for you?" (Matthew 20:32).

- Next ask them, "Do you believe Jesus is able to heal you?" (Matthew 9:28).

- And, "If Jesus is willing to heal you at this time, will you accept His healing now and in the way He chooses to bring it?" (Mark 1:40-42).[4]

- If it is appropriate, ask, "May I place my hands on your shoulder as we pray?"

- If the answers to the above questions are all yes, pray for them in a manner similar to the following:

*We agree Lord Jesus, if this is what You desire to do at this time, we accept Your healing for (name) and say to (name of illness, etc.) be healed in the name of Jesus Christ. Anything opposed to God at work here, we cancel your influence and effects and command you to leave now in Jesus' Name. Come Holy Spirit, fill them with Your presence and*

---

4    In this passage the leper is saying to Jesus, "if you're willing, you can make me clean." He knew Jesus was able to heal him. His question was not about Jesus ability or power to heal, it was about His willingness. This particular question is addressed in the suggested intervention and also diffuses any particular or specific expectations about how or when Jesus will heal.

*light and completely restore every part of their being, in Jesus'*
*Name, Amen.*

Next ask them about what is happening, what they are experiencing, and what thoughts are coming to mind. If necessary, ask Jesus to reveal anything that would keep them from experiencing His healing and freedom. In Jesus' Name command anything hidden or hindering their healing to come into the light of Christ and His truth. Here we are asking the Lord to reveal if there are any contributing factors to their condition e.g., why are they not experiencing healing or freedom at this time? Again, after asking Jesus to reveal what is hindering their freedom or healing and using His authority to audibly command any hidden influences into the light, ask them what comes to mind and/or if there is anything they believe might be hindering their healing. Listen, then begin to test, explore, and resolve those things that are revealed in the light of God's truth and through the counsel of the Holy Spirit. Continue and persevere until there is healing and/or peace with some measure of understanding.

# 19

# FREEING THOSE WHO ARE OPPRESSED

## USE AND SETTING FOR APPLICATION

The following is an example of **testing** and resolving potential demonic influences that may be affecting a person and keeping them from knowing the truth and living in the freedom Christ has willed for them. This kind of intervention should be used **every time anyone, anywhere is prayed for or being ministered to** whether in evangelistic or any other type of ministry. It should be regarded as a routine test.

## PURPOSE AND DESCRIPTION

Assuming or projecting the idea that a problem, condition, or need is in some way demonic in nature; and addressing it without first testing it, is not only presumptuous but less than sensitive or loving. This intervention is designed to first test to see what part, if any, of the problem or condition is demonically influenced in some way; or if the person is in some way being affected directly or indirectly by such forces. The purpose here is to first test **if** something is hidden, rooted in a lie, of demonic origin, or has gained some inroad through opportunity, etc. Secondly, to resolve the matter if such a condition exists. At the same time our aim is to insure that a person's dignity is maintained and that there is order, peace resulting in the biblical fruit of freedom.

## APPLICATION

In each opportunity for personal ministry it is important to test and expose any potential influence of evil that may be affecting the person to whom you are ministering. For example:

*If there is any influence opposed to Christ that is affecting or keeping (name of person) from his/her freedom and healing, in Jesus' Name, I command you to come into the light of Christ to be revealed to (name of person's) mind. In Christ's Name, I restrain you and suspend your influence, and release them to know the truth that leads to freedom in Jesus' Name."*

Stop and ask them what they are thinking about or experiencing. In most instances it is necessary to have them renounce anything (thoughts, lies, experiences or influences) that are opposed to the truth. Have them renounce all influences of evil that may have taken advantage of them through what they have participated in or were even unwillingly a part of. Agree with them in prayer and use Christ's authority, *In Jesus' Name, I command all influences of evil to be bound, I cancel your effects and now send you to Christ for judgment.*

# 20

# WHAT TO DO WHEN YOU DON'T KNOW WHAT TO DO

## USE AND SETTING FOR APPLICATION

To be applied when you don't know what to do and/or when what you have been trying doesn't seem to be working, is taking too long, and/or doesn't make sense.

## PURPOSE AND DESCRIPTION

The purpose of this approach is simply to re-establish ones reliance on Jesus' Holy Spirit for counsel and direction. The goal is dependence on Jesus – to look to Him, seek Him, and inquire of the Lord to counsel and allow Him to do things His way. Sometimes in our frustration, passion, or persistence we unconsciously begin to rely on our own strength, experience, or resources. At times like this we may find that we are more driven rather than led in our efforts.

## APPLICATION

Gather together as one and in unity (agreement) and ask Jesus what to do. Pay attention to what comes to mind. Test it according to God's Word and in prayer. Act on it in faith. (Matthew 18:19,20; John 16:13,14)

Use the authority you have been given by Jesus to forbid the enemy's influence and to call His influences into the light of Christ and His truth. In regard to personal ministry, it is important to remember that for the most part, unresolved matters are the result of not having discovered the source or root of a person's problems, feelings and/or behavior patterns. Repeated thoughts, feelings, and behavior patterns most always have their beginning point somewhere in a person's past in a particular memory or experience. These must be resolved at their point of origin before experiencing a real sense of freedom in the present. Asking the Holy Spirit to reveal the things (feelings, thoughts, behaviors, etc.) at their root, as well as using Christ's authority to call hidden and unresolved spiritual influences hindering one's freedom or knowledge of the truth into the light will enable the person to be aware of and understand the source of the problem or influence.

Gather together in unity and ask Jesus what to do. Pay attention to what comes to mind. Test it according to God's Word and in prayer. Act on it in faith.

After discovering the root of the problem or where the lie or influence was first introduced, it is then necessary for a person to resolve these according to God's Word and in keeping with the nature of the influence. For example, a person may need to forgive someone who has hurt them, and/or renounce an influence, lie, or effect that came through a particular experience or act of unrighteousness. One may need to verbally admit the truth while rejecting lies and renouncing the influences of a particular belief, feeling, or perception of themselves and/or the way things are.

The key is to always inquire of the Lord, utilize His authority to address those things that oppose God's will and truth. Then we must respond in obedience to God by submitting to His truth and resolving not to do anything apart from Him or until we have His clear counsel and direction.

It is also important for us to persevere until there are breakthroughs and freedom. It also helps to know that ongoing and repeated thoughts, feelings and/or patterns of negative behavior always have a point of introduction and need to be resolved.

For more on how to identify and resolve negative behaviors, patterns of thinking, and emotions at their point of origin please see notes, resources, and training opportunities for "Leading Others To Freedom" at www.**Kingdom**Ministries**Intl**.org

# 21

# INTERVENTIONS AND APPLICATIONS FOR DELIVERANCE MINISTRY AND ENGAGING IN SPIRITUAL WARFARE

## USE AND SETTING FOR APPLICATION

The following intervention is intended for settings of personal ministry and where you suspect a breakthrough is being contested by the influence of something demonic in nature. It may be used as a more intentional and provocative approach to testing and resolving demonic influences that you suspect are involved or remain hidden.

## PURPOSE AND DESCRIPTION

Most of the spiritual interventions you will be part of helping others resolve will have to do with the lies they believe and the false patterns of thinking (strongholds) that have accumulated over time. However, like the ministry of Jesus and the disciples there will be occasions where you will encounter demonic manifestations in various forms. Most of the time these will not be as obvious or as dramatic as some of the encounters we see in Scripture. The following are some things to be aware of and some suggestions for dealing with demonic influences.

## APPLICATION

First, foremost, and regardless of any feelings (fear, etc.), or dramatic activity, it is important to verbally (aloud, if possible) submit to God – look to Him and rely

Because Satan's influence is often hidden and subtle, it is important to test consistently by utilizing Christ's authority introduced by the word **IF.**

on Him in dependence by verbally asking for His help, presence and counsel; then resist the devil by using Christ's authority to verbally bind and suspend all activity of the evil one. Your goal here is to establish order by setting the terms or *ground rules* or the boundaries for what will and what will not happen; to **insure safety**, and enable the person you are praying for to respond, maintain their dignity and secure their freedom.

Because Satan's influence is often hidden and subtle with little indication of a recognizable manifestation, it is important to test consistently as described in this handbook by regularly utilizing Christ's authority introduced by the word "if". For example: *IF, there is any influence opposed to Christ, we suspend it's activity, expose it and separate it from any part of this person or issue to be seen in the light of Christ and His truth.* We recommend and encourage this kind of intervention whenever praying or ministering to anyone on any and all occasions.

If the response to this type of intervention provokes a manifestation or the individual reports or suspects that something demonic is affecting them, we suggest that first you bind (silence, restrain, render powerless) the activity/ spirit before attempting to cast it out in Jesus' Name.

With the spirit or influence bound and the activity suspended, *command* it to come into the light of Christ and to be subject to His truth to reveal how it got there and why it remains (what false claim it makes, reason or occasion for entry). At the same time, ask the Holy Spirit to reveal the source of the influence or why the influence or spirit is there and what is necessary for freedom. It is important to do this before prematurely *casting it out* so that the final condition is not worse than the first (Luke 11:26f). It's also important for the individual to know why and how it got there in order that they are not susceptible to the same type of bondage again.

If the influence still persists then deal with it directly by verbally commanding: *In the name of Jesus, I command that you tell me your name and by what right do you claim to be here.* Only obtain enough information to determine what right it claims and through what opportunity it gained entrance.

> Ask Jesus to reveal what needs to be done so that once the spirit or influence leaves, it will not be able to return. See sample prayer below.

Ask Jesus to reveal what needs to be done so that once the spirit or influence leaves, it will not be able to return. Pray something like, *Lord Jesus, we agree with (name) who wants to be free from this spirit, its effects, and to any possibility of its return. Will you please show him/her what needs be done to insure their freedom and healing.*

Ask them to report what comes to mind and discern together how the Holy Spirit is directing you. Carry out the instructions Jesus gives and follow-up to insure accountability.

Whenever possible, allow the person you are praying for to reject the influence themselves and command it to go in Jesus' Name. Doing this fosters empowerment in Christ Jesus and encourages discipleship in regard to maintaining their freedom.

**For acts of unrighteousness** that the person being ministered to has participated in or even experienced unwillingly through the unrighteous acts or influences of others, even by association and proximity (e.g., an environment of unrighteousness where they may have been affected) they will in most

> *In Jesus' Name, we fill every place the presence of evil was located with the Holy Spirit's presence and seal each of these areas in Christ for complete healing and restoration.*

cases need to renounce or reject any influence that may have taken the opportunity to affect them spiritually. According to **2 Corinthians 4:2** *"We have **renounced** secret and shameful ways"* which includes things they have participated in or deeds done to them, (sin committed or committed against them, acts of unrighteousness, sexual unions, traumatic experiences, forms of idolatry, evil influences through association with things or people, etc.).

In regard to acts of unrighteousness: Have the prayer recipient repeat after you as you say, *In Jesus' Name, I renounce (cut off) all spiritual influences associated with*

_____ .

*And, in Jesus' Name, I cancel all effects and influences that came about through, or as a result of_____ .*

The prayer minister then says something like, *In the name of Jesus Christ I now command you, unclean spirit, to* **take all of your effects** *and* **leave his/her body** *now as I send you* **to Christ** *for His judgment.*

The prayer team should now agree together that the place where any spirit or demonic influence affected them be restored, healed, and filled with the presence of Christ. The prayer minister can pray something like: *In Jesus' Name, we fill every place the presence of evil was located and/or influenced with the Holy Spirit's presence and seal each of these areas in Christ for complete healing and restoration. We agree together and say in agreement, (name) be restored and filled with the Holy Spirit, in Jesus' Name.*

If there is demonic activity, don't assume the person will be fine if a spirit leaves. Instant freedom from a spirit or spirits does not mean instant healing. However, you can expect that there is freedom from the demonic influence that a particular spirit or influence has had. Healing on the other hand, may take time and in some cases years because it is aimed at restoring the original wounds and root issues that provided the opportunity for Satan to take advantage. For more on how to identify and resolve negative behaviors, patterns of thinking, and emotions at their point of origin please see notes, resources, and training opportunities for "Leading Others To Freedom" at www.**Kingdom**Ministries**Intl**.org

We also discourage you or anyone else on your ministry team from ever declaring or stating that someone is free. That is something for them to give witness to after they see and experience the fruit of their freedom. In other words, let them tell you and look for the fruit that results from true freedom.

When the person receiving prayer shares what happened, it is important to avoid responding in any way that may appear as though you are shocked or judgmental. Never say, "I can't believe that you did that" or "No one would ever do something like that to you," or "that's a lie," "you did that (or feel that) because . . .," etc. Also, as best as you can, do not show facial expressions of disbelief or disapproval. Believe what they say! Even if you can't believe it, or find it difficult to believe what they are saying, it is important to respond to them as a person that is sharing what they perceive, experience, or feel is true. The Holy Spirit will reveal what's true if you rely on Him and His counsel. Never insinuate that someone is making something up – time and the Holy Spirit's truth will tell.

# 22

# THE PRINCIPLE OF CHRIST'S SOVEREIGN RULE⁵

## SETTING FOR APPLICATION

In settings where evangelistic outreach, missionary efforts, the establishment of a church;  or where ministry and prayer efforts are conducted in new and foreign regions.

## PURPOSE AND DESCRIPTION

The Principle of Christ's Sovereign Rule (CSR) is an effective approach to one particular aspect of spiritual warfare. This application of CSR is particularly useful in environments where one suspects cultural religious activity is prevalent (prayers, rituals, ceremonies, curses, food and/or other sacrifices, worship or reliance on other gods, idols, shamans, or various occult powers); and where regional (territorial) powers of darkness are suspected of being employed to interfere with the proclamation and advancement of the Kingdom of God, and the well-being of those who serve the Lord Jesus Christ in various forms of ministry.

---

5    The following is a revised application of the principle of RULE of the VICTOR (ROV) adopted from an anonymous source.  I am indebted to James Friesen, PhD who passed this on to me in a time of need. It has literally and absolutely transformed many situations for the glory of God and the advancement of His Kingdom.  It has also been instrumental in securing Christ's victory, our protection and the protection of those we love and to whom we minister. For more complete teaching on Christ Sovereign Rule (CSR) please visit our Resource Section at www.**Kingdom**MinistriesIntl.org

Settings where the application of CSR is useful include environments where cultists are suspected of employing anti-Christian, pagan religious practices, satanic rituals and/or the use of spiritual powers of darkness to disrupt Christ-centered ministry, churches, personal counseling, gatherings for worship and the proclamation of the Gospel. This includes spiritistic cultures as well as various expressions of cultural religion where occult practices and power are adhered to and used whether maliciously intended or not.

## DESCRIPTION

In the course of local church, faith-based, and cross-cultural ministry we have found that cultists were using various forms of pagan religious practice and/or satanic rituals to send (demonic) spirits in order to disrupt the work of the Church, affect Christian leaders, hinder the work of Christ-centered ministries, missionary efforts, and the proclamation of the Gospel. As the Holy Spirit made us aware of this activity, through His grace of discernment and through those who were being affected, we first began to bind these spirits, forbid their activity and send them to Christ for His judgment.

In time we discovered that this same process would be repeated frequently with the same cultist sending spirits each time. We have found that each time spirits were sent and we dealt with them authoritatively in the name of Christ, there would be noticeable and effective change.

As a result the cultists would increasingly face defeat and lose a measure of their power to send spirits. Over a period of time and after consistently utilizing the name and power of Christ, the battle seemed to be stripping them of power. In response, however, the cultists would increase their activity by continuing to use various rituals to gain more demonic power in an attempt to replace that which they had lost. Furthermore, they would enlist the support of other cultists in their personal network. Sometimes the enlisted cultists and their network would send spirits directly to their intended target; and at other times they would transfer the power to the cultist in need. Faced with this scenario, it became obvious to us that we were involved in a very real battle. Satan was using cultists to attack our ministry, us, and those we were ministering to, with demonic spirits. Although harassed, we, to a large degree, continued to be successful in our efforts to carry out the ministry God had called us to. Several issues however, bothered us. They were:

The principle of Christ Sovereign Rule is not a substitute for intercessory prayer. Rather, it is a declaration and a command to and against the powers of darkness.

- Being strictly limited to a defensive, reactionary posture.

- A defensive posture like this could never really be considered a victory. Such a posture was inconsistent with the overwhelming victory of Christ over evil through His death, resurrection and exaltation.

- The inability to stop the cultists or the effects of cultural religious practices from continuing their spiritual attacks against us to affect our personal well-being and effectiveness in ministry and relationships.

- In Christ, having been given His authority and promises, we should be able to stop any effort opposing Christ and His Kingdom in any attempt to advance the Kingdom of darkness (Luke 10:19b; Colossians 2:10).

- This is the concept behind the "Christ's Victorious Rule." It is not merely a prayer, although our ministry must always and continue to be rooted in prayer.

The principle of CSR is not a substitute for intercessory prayer. Rather, it is a statement – a declaration and a command to and against the powers of darkness based on:

- Christ's exalted position at the right hand of the Father, having been given all authority in heaven and on earth (Matthew 28:18; Colossians 2:10 NLT).

- The power and authority He has given to those who believe (Matthew 10:1, 5-7; 16:19; Mark 16:16-18; Luke 9:1-2; 9,17; 10:1-2; John 14:12-14).

- His expressed purpose and will to overcome evil through His Body the Church (Ephesians 3:10).

- Our position in Christ as His children, heirs, citizens, soldiers and agents of His Kingdom who are given authority over all the power of the enemy with Jesus' promise to keep us from harm (provided we use the authority He's given us and remain in Him) (Luke 10:19; Psalm 91).

- His command to go into all the world with His authority and power (Matthew 28:18-20; Acts 1:8).

- The principles of biblical spiritual warfare illustrated throughout Scripture.

## SPECIFIC APPLICATIONS

**MISSIONS:** particularly in spiritistic or other dark cultures where occult powers are used, (witch doctor, shaman, Imam, etc.) If there is a spiritual attack by this cultic power upon the missionary or his/her ministry, CSR may be applied. Regional cultic powers will seek to interfere with any evangelistic or church planting effort. Continued application of CSR will free the region's populace in order that those you are ministering to might hear and respond to the Gospel and the ministry of Jesus through you.

**CHURCH/PASTORAL:** If Satan and the powers of darkness are interested in hindering the advancement of God's Kingdom and the Gospel of Jesus Christ, it is quite possible, in fact, there is evidence to support that cultists pray and even infiltrate churches to various degrees of involvement specifically for the spiritual disruption and defeat of local church ministries and pastors. CSR could and, at times, should be regularly applied for pastors and/ or leaders prior to the start of services or when initiating ministries and various forms of outreach conducted by local churches.

**SPECIAL GATHERINGS OR CONFERENCES:** Where the Gospel and God's truth is presented, e.g., evangelistic outreaches, gatherings for corporate prayer and/ or worship, "prayer summits", spiritual warfare conferences, pastor's/leadership conferences, mission's conferences, marriage conferences, etc.

> The statement of Christ Sovereign Rule is a declaration made from our position in Christ and the authority He gives to the Body of Christ and the individual believer.

**HIGH PROFILE MINISTRIES:** Focus on the Family, Promise Keepers, Evangelism Explosion, Billy Graham Conferences, etc.

**PERSONAL MINISTRY:** In settings where personal ministry (counseling, prayer ministry) is engaged. CSR is particularly essential in ministering to those who have a history of occult involvement, ritual abuse, and/or who are breaking free from cultural religious and family influences that are antagonistic toward Christ and the Gospel.

The statement of CSR is again a declaration made from our position in Christ and the authority He gives to the Body of Christ and the individual believer. We believe it is best utilized in a team, where two or more are gathered in His Name (Matthew 18:19-20). It is not a ritual nor is it to be used as such. It is only effective if it is done in humility; and where one is dependent on the empowerment of God's Spirit, with full awareness that we stand only in Christ's accomplished victory using His authority to promote God's purpose and will. In this regard we must be forthright and intentional in our declaration of CSR. Just saying the words is not only unfruitful but potentially harmful.

## APPLICATION

**CHRIST'S SOVEREIGN RULE:** The following declaration is best utilized where two or more are gathered in Christ's Name and when it is asserted audibly and in agreement with others in the Body of Christ. It may be necessary to employ CSR on more than one occasion as together you discern and intercede for Christ's victory in the particular setting you're in:

*In Jesus' Name, I (we) assert the resurrected Lordship and dominion of the Lord Jesus Christ over every region, power, gathering, or person that is purposed against (name, group, type of ministry, etc.) and over every region that has permitted or is permitting spirits in or through their territories or is being invoked against us or the purpose and will of Jesus Christ.*

*In the name of the Lord Jesus Christ, I (we) command that they be cut off and forbidden from ever receiving power from darkness again. I (we) command the immediate transfer of all their resources from the Kingdom of darkness into the Kingdom of light for the purpose of their defeat; the honor and victory of Christ and the complete restoration of all things that have been affected or hindered.*

*In Jesus' Name, and with the authority and power He has given us over all the powers of darkness we forbid any harm or hindrance to God's purpose for us and through us; we destroy all of your magical arts, books, and sorcery along with every means you use to invoke evil; we revoke every assignment purposed against us and cut off all connections associated with evil. Together we render you powerless and cancel every ritual, curse, hex, or spell, and all their effects. We command the immediate reversal of all your schemes and send you now to Christ for judgment.*

*In Jesus' Name, we say that the hand of the Lord is against you now and we subject you to His power, will, and punishment. We disband the gatherings of those subject to the powers of darkness whether knowingly or unknowingly and render powerless all their activity in order that all may know that Jesus Christ is Lord of all. We forbid any form of retaliation and now claim God's complete protection and restoration. With Jesus we claim and together pray, "Father, thy Kingdom come and thy will be done now on earth as it is in heaven." We ask for and claim the presence of God, His peace, power, and counsel to carry out His will in righteousness and truth.*

*I (we) submit every part of my/our being to Christ alone who is our fortress and strength. In Jesus' Name. Amen*

# SECTION IV

CLOSING REMARKS AND
GETTING IN TOUCH

CONCLUSION

Thank you for purchasing this Field Guide and for your willingness to rely on the Lord Jesus Christ in applying the tools and interventions included in this handbook. Again, we would like to encourage you and those with whom you gather and fellowship to test and apply this material as needed in the various situations and ministry endeavors in which you are involved. Relying on Jesus through the counsel of the Holy Spirit and utilizing Christ's authority along with the resources God provides through the Body of Christ is central for the effective application of these tools, for discipleship, and the advancement of God's Kingdom.

If you have questions or testimonies you would like to share in response to using the material that's provided here, please send them by email to kingdommail@**Kingdom**Ministries**Intl**.org or through our website www.**Kingdom**Ministries**Intl**.org. You can also find us on social media by searching Kingdom Ministries and Counseling Center, Fresno, CA.

If you are interested in hosting or helping to organize a conference or seminar for further training utilizing this material or one of our ministry training workshops, a speaking engagement or event, please contact our offices at the above email addresses or call in the U.S. 559.226.2750. Our mailing address is 245 West Shaw Avenue, Fresno, CA 93704 – U.S.A.

# APPENDIX

## ATYPICAL RESPONSES TO PRAYER
## MINISTRY, FREEDOM AND INNER HEALING

In the course of praying for others you will encounter persons for whom prayer ministry does not seem to be as effective or fruitful as it is for some others you've prayed for. There can be a number of reasons for this that include unresolved psychological, physical, and/or emotional issues. However, due to the scope of this handbook we would like to point out two significant areas for testing and discernment that you are likely to encounter as you become more involved in this type of ministry. The first has to do with chemical imbalances in the brain and other forms of mental illness. The second has to do with the unconscious ability to dissociate from painful memories or uncomfortable experiences in the present.

According to the Scriptures we understand that all human beings are made in the image of God – a complex and integrated whole of mind, body, and spirit. We also understand that human behavior is the result of a combination of influences including environmental (cultural, sociological, familial), psychological, and spiritual forces (Ephesians 2:1-3). Consequently behavior is often not a symptom of just one of these influences but a combination of some or all of them. Therefore it is important that each of these areas be tested and treated.

Depression for example, can result from emotional and psychological influences as a result of a significant loss or a sustained period of difficulty. Another type of depression can be a symptom of physical pain, suffering or an extended period of illness. As the body is affected so are our emotions and spirit. Over time this kind of physical depression leads to emotional depression as well. Clinical depression is a mental illness due to complex factors including chemical and hormonal imbalances. This kind of depression is a medical condition and not a weakness, or something you can simply "snap out" of or be "delivered" from. It is a chronic illness that usually requires long-term treatment, like diabetes or high blood pressure. Unless the Lord chooses to heal this particular type of depression it will otherwise need to be treated with medication designed to restore the body's normal function.

Depression can also be spiritual in nature. At a very basic level it can affect our human spirit and attitudes toward God, faith, others and our outlook on life in general. There may also be a demonic component to depression. This type of depression comes as the result of some kind of demonic influence taking advantage of an existing circumstance, condition, type of depression, false belief, or unresolved area of vulnerability. At times depression may simply be an outright attack of the enemy to promote discouragement and hopelessness as we see in the case of Job. The good news is that this type of depression in any form is the easiest to treat and the first step toward resolving any of the other types.

Depression is further complicated when one or more types of depression occur simultaneously. To make matters worse, demonic influences can contribute to any one or all of these areas of vulnerability. Again, this underscores the importance of testing and encouraging the Prayer Recipient (PR) to pursue the treatment of all related areas through the counsel of the Holy Spirit and by testing and resolving any demonic influences. This will free the individual to pursue and receive the help they need without the unnecessary influence of the Evil One.

Again, the topic of depression here is only used to illustrate that any human condition or problem is likely to include more than a single source or influence that needs to be tested, treated and resolved because we are complex beings – a workmanship created in Christ Jesus.

## MENTAL ILLNESS

Mental illness is generally described as any disease or condition affecting the brain that influences the way a person thinks, feels, behaves, and/or relates to others and to his or her surroundings. A medical diagnosis of mental illness generally is based one or more conditions that cause a significant amount of distress in your life to the point that it hinders your ability to function at work, home, in relationships or other social situations. There are more than 200 conditions classified as mental illnesses, ranging from minor to severe. Common mental illnesses include depression and schizophrenia.    Again because we are beings created in the image of God – an integrated whole of mind, body, and spirit it is important to recognize there may be more than one issue contributing to a person's problem and freedom.   For example, a person who has difficulty completing projects, is disorganized and lives a life characterized by what others would describe as chaos and disorder, may not have unresolved trauma from their past or an "evil spirit" of some kind. While they could be affected by something demonic they may simply have a condition known as Attention Deficit Disorder.   While prayer ministry can certainly help, it may require medical treatment unless of course the Lord heals this condition outright.

For now, there are two types of mental illness in particular that one should be aware of when involved in prayer ministry – Bipolar Disorder and Schizophrenia. For our purpose as prayer ministers it is important to understand that we are not to identify or diagnose any type of condition or disorder.  Neither are we to suggest it.  We may however suggest an evaluation by trained professionals who are qualified to do so.  Particularly if it's something that is prayed about and tested with the individual you are praying for and they agree that it is the counsel of the Holy Spirit.  For now it will suffice to be aware of some basic symptoms and to remain alert to the possibility of mental illness when a typical approach to resolving root issues in prayer is not effective.

At a very basic and unscientific level we've made the following observations in regard to mental illness in general and in regard to Bipolar Disorder and Schizophrenia in particular:

**Observation #1 - When the Prayer Recipient (PR) reports hearing voices either during or outside the setting for prayer ministry.**

This kind of report should be adequately tested in regard to the root or source of the voices as described in this handbook. Generally there are three possibilities you should be aware of. One is that the voices are demonic – internal and/or external. Two, the voices are external, audible and heard only by the person reporting them even in a public place. This kind is more characteristic of someone who may have symptoms of Schizophrenia. Three, the voices are internal, distinct, intelligible, have personality and age-appropriate characteristics – tone of voice and vocabulary of an adolescent or toddler for example. Bodily movements, expressions, interests, and actions that are uncharacteristic of an adult. The latter condition is characteristic of someone who has the ability to dissociate as the result of a hyper-traumatic past (this will be explained later in the appendix).

**Observation #2 - When the PR has unusually detailed and grandiose visions, images, and graphic scenes they report when they share their experiences with you and/or during the time they report to you after praying for them.**

This sometimes is characteristic of those with Bipolar Disorder. However, there are many spiritually gifted individuals who "see" very clear and graphic pictures and images that come from God. There are also demonic influences that project graphic and detailed images. Others may in fact be describing the hallucinatory effects of a past memory where the individual was drugged or under the influence of a particular substance.

Even with testing, as described in this handbook, it is sometimes difficult to discern. However, this is where you along with others on the team, and/or professionals are important in discerning what is of God and what is of human or satanic origin and what may be some form of mental illness. Complicating the matter even further is that true spiritual gifting or revelation from God may be embellished and distorted as a result of the mental illness. In addition, demonic influences can take advantage of the vulnerabilities of the mental illness. Once more, the first priority is to restrain, suspend and forbid demonic influences in Christ's Name. Secondly, test and discern the images and as the Scripture says, "hold onto what is good and avoid that which is evil." There may be some "gold" amidst the sand. After awhile you will be able to recognize the kinds of things that God reveals – the way He reveals things will always be consistent with the way He reveals things in His Word. Most of all the things that come from God will bear fruit and they will lead you on the path to freedom and healing. The images, pictures, and revelations that come from God are pieces of a larger puzzle. Like Jesus' parables they have a single point and provide some direction. By contrast mental illness or the enemy will bring confusion, promote distraction and focus on the detail, i.e, analyzing the bark on a tree instead of seeing the forest and the path through it.

**Observation #3 – When the PR repeatedly brings up a particular issue again and again following the process of testing and resolving the same issue. For example, one individual referred to us by a pastor would on various occasions come forward following a Sunday morning church service in response to an "altar call" to receive Christ.**

This happened numerous times before Prayer Teams and others recognized this pattern and the individual was referred for prayer ministry to try and resolve her uncertainty regarding salvation. Despite having sincerely confessing Jesus as Lord and believing in her heart that God raised Him from the dead, repenting of all known sin, declaring and agreeing wholeheartedly with the a variety of Scriptures assuring her of her salvation, and renouncing any lies or feelings contradicting God's Word, she would repeatedly get stuck on her uncertainty and return to it. Thankfully she agreed to an evaluation and her diagnosis and subsequent treatment was consistent with mental illness. Her behavior stopped and her symptoms subsided as long as she remained consistent with her medication.

## SUICIDAL THOUGHTS/TENDENCIES

Whether it's someone you know or someone you are praying for it is important to take any talk or indications of suicide seriously. While you as a volunteer prayer minister are not required by law to report something like this we do encourage you to let a qualified person know – a counselor, psychiatrist pastor, suicide hot-line phone counselor, teacher, or other professional--when you suspect the individual is in real danger of harming themselves or others. As nonprofessionals we recommend the following interventions:

## APPLICATION

First and foremost, pray with them in person or by phone in the following manner even if they don't agree or are unable to respond something like:

*Lord Jesus I ask you to be present for and with _____ right now. Let your power and dominion be manifest there, over this situation, and over their mind, body, emotions and over every power and authority that opposes the Lord Jesus Christ and the abundant life that He wills for them. And, in Jesus' Name, I command that all powers and influences present or promoting anything that opposes the will and purpose of the Lord Jesus Christ be bound, silent, and to leave now with their effects in Jesus' Name. I assert Christ's dominion over their mind, emotions, and will and suspend all unresolved influences that are contributing to their condition at this time. I ask you Lord Jesus to command your angels concerning _____ to guard them in all of their ways and lead us into the truth that brings freedom. Holy Spirit I ask that you would reveal the truth they need to know from you right now and the good plans you have for their future. I release them to know the truth and the outcome of the choices before them and free them to respond to Christ as He is at work in them to will and to do what He desires, in Jesus' Name.*

After this kind of initial intervention, stop and ask them to verbalize anything they are experiencing as a result of your prayer for them. The immediate goal here is NOT to try and resolve a root issue as you would in other settings. The foremost objective is to insure their safety and free them from any influence that would keep them from hearing and responding to Jesus and taking the steps they need to be safe and get the help they need.

As soon as you are able to get their participation with you ask them to make a verbal promise to you that they will not harm themselves or anyone else without speaking in person and praying with you first.

Furthermore, ask them to please repeat after you something like the following prayer: *Lord Jesus, even though I feel hopeless and cannot see any reason for living. I give up control of my life to you — whether you choose to take my life or allow me to live. I surrender my will to yours and renounce any opening I've given to the Evil One and reject his influence in any form in Jesus' Name. I ask for your help, protection, and hope. Restore my mind and align my feelings with your truth. I submit them to you now and give you alone the right to rule in matters concerning my life. I agree with you and my friend not to harm myself or anyone else. Even though I don't feel like it's true, I agree that your truth is "your plans for me are good, to give me hope and a future." Let it be so according to your Word. Amen.*

Follow this up by confirming that they will agree to what they said and will promise to keep their commitment until you have the opportunity to talk with them in person.

## DISSOCIATIVE ABILITIES

In the world of professional behavioral science this condition is referred to as Dissociative Identity Disorder (DID). DID is characterized by the expression of two or more distinct personality states or identities that repeatedly or at various times exert control of an individual's behavior. These "personalities" can exhibit a variety of age-specific behaviors and corresponding age-appropriate verbal and bodily characteristics. Each personality state can have a separate name and exhibit a distinct identity, persona, and personal history. These alternate identities frequently display different and contrasting characteristics to that of the primary individual – hostile, self-destructive, controlling, etc. In addition, alternate identities "switch" or take control often in sequence or at times as the result of an emotional, physiological, spiritual, or environmental "trigger" – a loud noise, fear, pain, etc.

An individual personality state also holds and represents specific memories and emotions of a particular segment of time in the person of origin's life. The person of origin or host personality refers to the one named at birth and the one to whom others refer to by their given or birth name. This core personality is characteristically passive, dependent, guilty and depressed.

Another key attribute of a person with DID is the inability to recall important personal information that is beyond what is attributed to ordinary forgetfulness. The individual or others may report incidents where there is a "loss of time" – the inability to account for extended blocks of time from hours to even days.

We understand DID to be primarily an ability to survive and cope with extreme trauma and abuse by separating (dissociating) from the original event in order to survive physically and emotionally. We believe this ability to survive is something God gives as a temporary provision in order for the body and mind to survive extreme and sustained trauma including devastating physical, psychological, and emotional and/or ritual abuse. It is given to postpone the effects of trauma until there is safety and the resources necessary to heal and recover. Without this ability the individual simply would cease to live or function normally. This gift or ability however, becomes a liability when the individual continues to rely on their ability to dissociate after the period of abuse and danger is over. However, the person who dissociates does not necessarily do so deliberately. It is often an unconscious, automatic and/or programmed response. This ongoing cycle and reliance on dissociation subsequent to the period of trauma is the primary barrier to healing and the enjoyment of life and healthy relationships as God intended. God's purpose and will is for each person to be whole and free to enjoy the abundant life He intended and promised, and to fulfill the purpose He created and gifted them for.

What to look for and how to respond to those either diagnosed with DID or who appear to exhibit symptoms:

- As a Prayer Minister you are not responsible or qualified to diagnose someone with DID. We strongly encourage you to avoid any identification or labeling of someone's perceived condition. The following is provided only to assist you in recognizing and working with those who may demonstrate dissociative behaviors or are properly diagnosed with DID. The purpose here is to make some sense of what may be occurring in the lives of some of those you pray with when prayer ministry or other attempts to minister or care result in confusion and difficulty. We also hope to avert "blaming the victim" or improperly judging a person's motive or desire to receive help when nothing you try seems to work.

- As with any person created in the image of God, respond with love and understanding. Perhaps the most important thing you can do is to listen and respond to their story with compassion and belief. You may find it hard to believe what is happening or the things being described. Whether you believe it or not the issue is to remain reliant on the Holy Spirit to reveal the truth to you and the person you are ministering to. Our role is to allow Him to be the judge and reveal truth to them and for us to follow His lead and not our own perceptions.

- You may initially notice that the individual you're praying with can't recall moments or extended periods of time. For example, they may not be able to recall what you said or prayed. They may also speak and act like a different person and speak in a different tone of voice. They may speak and act like a younger child and demonstrate consistent childlike characteristics and actions. Or they may be belligerent, defiant, and argumentative like a troubled adolescent, for example. We've found it helpful to respond as if you would to a person of that age and to ask them what they are experiencing or if they have any questions.

- In your initial encounters there will likely be lots of confusing responses, behavior, and events that don't seem to add up or make sense. In addition, there will be an unusual amount of demonic spiritual activity that will seek to hinder your progress and affect their wellbeing especially during times of ministry.

- If you suspect you're dealing with a dissociative person or the individual you're praying with indicates they have a history or diagnosis of DID it is of foremost importance that you help them feel safe and create a place of safe environment for them.

- It is both helpful and insightful to ask a few key questions to help them orient themselves and help you identify what's going on. We suggest questions like, "Do you know where you are? What is today's date and year? What is your name? The answers to these questions will often reveal the personality state that's in control at the moment. They may insist they are presently in a place (geographical location) and time that is actually part of the host person's past. In other words they believe the date to be a time other than the present day, time and year. These type of responses are indicative of the memories the alter personality experienced and those that the host cannot remember. These are the memories and wounds that need to be resolved.

- Before you or others determine that dissociative behaviors are demonic they should be wisely tested and discerned. Certainly there are times a person will seem to manifest demonic behavior and characteristics. Sometimes in fact they can look the same. It is therefore important to test, discern and respond to whatever is being manifest with a consistent calm manner and tone of voice. There is no advantage to boisterous actions or tone of voice whether it's something demonic or not. The Word of God and the authority of Christ is what are effective for demonic influences. However, it is counterproductive and hurtful to treat an alter personality who is part of an individual made in God's image like an evil spirit. Besides, a personality state will not respond by leaving or being bound like a demon would, no more than a part of our personality can be "cast out." Rather, a personality will respond like a human being with a distinct age, personality, intellect and emotions.

- While the process of ministering freedom and healing by resolving root causes and spiritual influences is the same as it is with any other person you pray with, there are some important considerations and interventions that are unique to those with dissociative abilities. We would recommend the following as you begin this kind of ministry:

- An evaluation, diagnosis, and a consistent schedule of appointments with a licensed Christ-Centered counselor and psychiatrist who are experienced and knowledgeable about DID.

- We would recommend a basic primer on the subject for those in prayer ministry with those diagnosed with DID. Because we know Dr. James Friesen personally and have utilized his counsel on occasion for nearly 20 years we recommend some material he's written on the subject: *Uncovering the Mystery of MPD* by James G. Friesen.

- In addition, the most important and effective approach to ministering to someone with DID is to utilize the counsel of the Holy Spirit and Christ's authority with at least two or more in a team approach to ministry.

- Contact Kingdom Ministries or Counseling Center for support and team consultations at 559-226-2750 or **Kingdom**Ministries**Intl**.org

**At Kingdom Ministries we measure progress toward wholeness and freedom by the following indicators:**

- A consistent willingness to face the truth as Jesus reveals it and respond by doing what He says despite one's feelings, experiences, or thoughts to the contrary. The pursuit of healing and freedom along with a resolute commitment to trust and obey Jesus is a significant indicator of a person's investment in freedom. Discernment by the Holy Spirit and with others who rely on Him is necessary to establish healthy boundaries for yourself and other team members and to distinguish between the unintentional tendency of the DID person to depend on other people to meet all of their needs.

- Maintaining a consistent schedule of ministry, counseling, and team appointments.

- Consistent memory work – the resolution of memories where the person of origin (host personality) is submitted to Christ and responding to Him and what He reveals about what needs to be resolved in regard to different personality states. Memory resolution and healing involves the process of the host remembering and often experiencing the original event that was postponed and relegated to another personality in order to survive; the acknowledgement and acceptance of what happened, the feelings and effects that resulted. With this acceptance and acknowledgement the host takes on the memory of what was absorbed by the another personality and then releases it to Christ who bore our wounds on the cross. The healthy expression of feelings is critical to the healing process as well as educating the DID person about managing and understanding them. This is where the respective roles of a therapist and a psychiatrist are essential as these are generally beyond the scope of a prayer minister's role.

- Regular episodes of spiritual deliverance, covering and prayer are a key indicator of progress and an essential part of their freedom. The very nature of DID assumes an unusual history of abuse and trauma. Sadly, in a good many cases there is the added devastation of ritual abuse – religious and/or overtly satanic forms of abuse and programming (brainwashing). As a result memory work and ministry will include deliverance from demonic beings and the necessity of freedom from lies and false patterns of belief. It will also require a biblical and practical understanding of spiritual warfare to provide the kind of environment you and others will need to minister and live in freedom.

- Acknowledgement, acceptance of and care for the other personalities by the host are perhaps the most telling indicators of progress toward wholeness and freedom. This is especially true when this kind of relationship takes place outside the prayer or therapeutic environment. The goal here is for the host to restore trust and an interdependent relationship with the other personalities. This will not happen suddenly nor should there be too much expectation or pressure to make it happen. This again will come in response to their willingness to listen and follow the counsel of the Holy Spirit along with the help of those who are trained in this process. However, if there are not signs of progress in this key area it may time to re-evaluate your role with the individual through the process of team prayer and discernment.

CPSIA information can be obtained at www.ICGtesting.com
Printed in the USA
BVOW11s0811050314

346602BV00005BA/30/P